Many of us have our thoughts backward about life and death. John Owen, the great Puritan preacher and theologian, on his deathbed dictated a letter to a friend. The secretary had written, "I am yet in the land of the living. . . ." when Owen paused in midsentence, saying, "Stop! Change that. Write, 'I am yet in the land of the dying, but I hope soon to be in the land of the living.'"

Surely, this is the essence of our instinctive interest in the hereafter — an interest that is sending people today in search of answers from a wide variety of sources, many of which are mirages, if not demonic deceptions! Let's turn to the Scriptures and see what God has chosen to tell us about life after death.

After Death, What?

Gerald C. Studer
Introduction by
Paul Erb

HERALD PRESS
Scotdale, Pennsylvania
Kitchener, Ontario

AFTER DEATH, WHAT?
Copyright © 1976 by Herald Press, Scottdale, Pa. 15683
    Published simultaneously in Canada by Herald Press,
    Kitchener, Ont. N2G 1A7
Library of Congress Catalog Card Number: 75-38074
International Standard Book Number: 0-8361-1792-1
Printed in the United States of America
Design by Alice B. Shetler

Dedicated to
my wife, Marilyn,
my daughters, Jerri and Maria,
and to my parents,
Martin and Edna Studer

CONTENTS

AUTHOR'S PREFACE

"What in the world are you doing!" exclaimed a friend to a famous author as he found him writing page after page while sitting by the fire and consigning each to the flames. "Clearing my mind," was the firm and simple reply.

And so it is. In a similar effort to clear my mind, as well as to inform it, I have attempted to make a biblical study of the afterlife. I first presented these studies to my congregation at Scottdale, Pennsylvania. Though it is a difficult topic, I did so with confidence in both their interest and open-mindedness, not to mention candid reactions. At the time, I had no intention of reducing them to manuscript for a wider audience.

Had it not been for the persistent urging of Maynard W. Shetler, a division head of the Mennonite Publishing House who was also a member of the congregation, my notes would probably have been subsequently stashed away and forgotten. He travels widely in Christian circles and insisted that this series should be published both because of the interest among Christians and because of the occult revival. My reply was that if I had occasion to present the series again I would keep publication in mind.

I had scarcely settled in Lansdale, Pennsylvania, some months later when I was asked to lead an evening class of about one hundred adults through a series on the life beyond death. The members of this class were also eager students and astute questioners. The chapters of this book owe much to their interest and helpfulness, as well as to Paul M. Schrock's deft editorial skills. I am indebted also to Mrs. Dolores Kratz for her able deciphering of my rough drafts of shoddy manuscript and penciled-in notes.

I shall be rewarded if these studies stimulate readers to search the Scriptures for themselves. If such persons arrive at different conclusions, I shall still be satisfied, for I see this effort not so much as the end of a journey as an attempt to work in an area where our Lord has not left us teaching that is as clear and full as we might desire.

It remains for us in this life to love and obey Him knowing that He does all things well. May these pages give others an eagerness to enter into the wonders of that life to come. Bon voyage!

Gerald C. Studer, pastor
Plains Mennonite Church
Lansdale, Pennsylvania

October, 1975

INTRODUCTION

After Death, What? is another contribution to current discussions on eschatology, death, and the life beyond. It is biblical in its method, probing deeply into what the Bible really teaches. The author raises questions that many have not raised. Committed to a belief in a second coming of Christ at the end of this age, with such accompaniments as the resurrection and the judgment, he asks what happens to us between death and the return of Christ. He rejects the common idea that we go immediately to a final heaven or hell in favor of teachings on an intermediate state, which he calls the near hereafter. Many of us have heard little of any intermediate state, except for the Catholic concept of purgatory. But it is good to ask why there should be a judgment at the end of time if people have already been admitted into heaven or banished to hell.

Another question about the near hereafter concerns a possible unseen life which runs parallel to this earthly, historical existence. What Christian answer may there be, apart from demonic spiritism, to the various kinds of appearances and communications which are reported from time to time? Examples of these are the realities of another world sometimes glimpsed by dying people. Are the departed ones conscious of what is going on among us here? What is the communion of saints that our creeds and our hymns talk about?

And is the notion correct that suddenly at death we will be perfect and all-knowing? Or will learning continue in our near hereafter? And will the starting place be where we have arrived in this life? What growth in the Spirit will there be? Wouldn't a static perfection be monotonous and without challenge?

In meeting such questions the author seeks for scriptural answers. For he fully accepts that human philosophizing is futile, and that only the divinely revealed Word of God can tell us what lies beyond death. But the Word needs to be interpreted and understood. And not all readers may follow Studer in his interpretations. For instance, he takes the story of Dives and Lazarus, not as a parable, but as a realistic account of a happening. Indeed, he leans quite heavily on this story for facts about life after death. But there are scholars, just as much committed to scriptural authority, who see this story as a parable, and following the usual principles for interpreting parables, use the main thrust of this story without pressing too much on its details. So there are things in this section on the near hereafter which can be controversial.

The boundary between the near and the far hereafter is the parousia of Christ and its related developments. Some readers may have trouble with chapter 8, which is on hell. "The Dark Side of the Far Hereafter." The author's purpose is to keep his readers from making the Bible say more than it does. The main question is whether hell is unending. The author shows no disposition to reject anything that the Bible means and says.

We are here talking about the far hereafter, when time shall be no more, and we must all recognize the problems in bringing time concepts into the eternal state.

None of us wants to have any part in giving anyone the hope that men can reject God's salvation with anything less than eternal consequences. God is love, it is true; but He is also a consuming fire. A frown of judgment is just as much in place on the face of God as is a smile of approval. It has long seemed to me that any concept of universal salvation makes nonsense of a final judgment.

But cautions that some of us may feel on this point may seem less necessary when we read chapter 10 on "Probation in This Life," which may be taken as the author's summary position. Here he argues without danger of misunderstanding that "character tends to permanence," and that willful choice "determines one's destiny." There is a warning here that "darkness comes from willful choice," and no hint that condemnation in the judgment has a temporary effect.

This book should be read in an honest and unprejudiced search for biblical truth. The author asks for only this in his preface, and the conversation with him will be worthwhile even for those whose conclusions may be stated a bit differently.

Paul Erb
Scottdale, Pennsylvania

December 16, 1975

1

OUR LAST APPOINTMENT

"Heard about Joe?"

"Yeah!"

"Too bad, eh?"

"How old was he?"

"Fifty-two."

"Oh, well, when your time's up, ya gotta' go!"

This terse conversation between two Manhattan cab drivers sums up the average person's thoughts and attitudes toward death. Yet the fact is that the next major event for each of us will be our own death.

Asked to list life's major experiences, most people would mention marriage and parenthood, and perhaps taxes. But death is more universal and paramount than any of them. Some never marry. Not all become parents. Many never pay any taxes. But every individual, every last one of us, will die! It is indeed "appointed unto men once to die" (Heb. 9:27, KJV), as the Scripture says, unless the Lord returns first. A stray germ in a drop of water, a split-second wrong turn by someone on the highway, or the sudden stopping of our heart can end it all for any of us.

An old German proverb says, "As soon as a man is born he is old enough to die." Death is no respecter of persons. Even a child may lose a playmate or a grandparent.

Our forefathers spoke much more freely of death than we do. Walter Lippmann observed, "Our ancestors thought they knew their way from birth through eternity; we are puzzled about the day after tomorrow."

Dr. Gumpert of the Goldwater Memorial Hospital once commented that "paradoxical as it may seem, death is a vital function of our species. Can you imagine how unbearably sloppy life would be if all the causes of death were eliminated? The boredom would be monumental. Every day of the year we'd have to attend some relative's birthday. Nothing would be important or unimportant. There would be no stakes, physical, mental, or moral. Our conduct would have no meaning. Death does for us what the final curtain does for a play. It gives form to our existence."

Many of us have our thoughts backward about life and death. John Owen, the great Puritan preacher and theologian, on his deathbed dictated a letter to a friend. The secretary had written, "I am yet in the land of the living . . ." when Owen paused in midsentence, saying, "Stop! Change that. Write, 'I am yet in the land of the dying, but I hope soon to be in the land of the living.'"

Surely, this is the essence of our instinctive interest in the hereafter — an interest that is sending people today in search of answers from a wide variety of sources, many of which are mirages, if not demonic deceptions! Let's turn to the Scriptures and see what God has chosen to tell us about life after death.

Only two persons in all recorded history, Enoch and Elijah, have been spared the inevitable appointment with death. And the details of these two great escapes are exceedingly meager. All we're told concerning Enoch is that he "walked with God; and he was not, for God took him" (Gen. 5:24). Of Elijah we are simply informed that as he and Elisha "still went on and talked, behold, a chariot of fire and horses of fire separated the two of them. And Elijah went up by a whirlwind into heaven. . . . And Elisha . . . saw him no more" (2 Kings 2:11, 12).

Only a few persons have ever returned from the dead. These include (1) Jairus' daughter, (2) an unnamed widow's son, (3) Lazarus, (4) those who came forth from their graves at the time of Christ's resurrection, and (5) such persons as Dorcas in New Testament times and perhaps a few in subsequent centuries. But all of these soon died again anyway! [1]

Only one person ever returned from the dead never to die again. That was Christ! His defeat of death gives hope to all of us, as He said, "He who believes in me, though he die, yet shall he live, and whoever lives and believes in me shall never die" (Jn. 11:25, 26).

But for the mass of mankind since the dawn of creation the logic in the soliloquy of Hamlet reigns supreme. Hamlet, reflecting upon the burdens and toils of life, muses that no one would struggle to prolong life

> But that the dread of something after death,
> The undiscover'd country from whose bourn
> No traveler returns, puzzles the will
> And makes us rather bear those ills we have
> Than fly to others we know not of? [2]

Before Christ came, the prospects beyond the grave were vague indeed. Alan Richardson tersely characterizes the situation before Christ when he says:

> The Bible never for one moment allows men to forget their mortality: man is akin to God, he is "visited" by God, yet he differs from God in that he shares . . . mortality with the beasts that perish (Ps. 144:3, 4; 49, *passim*). The illusion of natural or inherent immortality is the Serpent's lie (Gen. 3:4). The Hebrews, like other primitive peoples, . . . [regarded death as]. . . joining the departed souls in the underworld (Sheol), a dreary, meaningless existence where one was cut off from "the land of the living" and from the presence of Jehovah (*cf.* Ps. 88:10-12 and many other passages). [3]

The first territory which Abraham acquired in the land that God had promised him was a burial plot (Gen. 23:1-20). Joshua could console himself and his fellow Israelites with little more than the words, "And now I am about to go the way of all the earth" (Josh. 23:14). The wise woman of Tekoa who came to David could only say, "We must all die, we are like water spilt on the ground, which cannot be gathered up again" (2 Sam. 14:14).

True, the Old Testament contains many passages that speak of death with a calm moderation because of the writer's confidence in God's steadfast love toward those who keep His covenant (Ps. 103: 15-18, for example).

The Israelites did not indulge in much speculation on precisely where the dead go. There was a general belief that those who died went to a place beyond God's reach, the abode of the dead, separated from God, incapable of serving Him or praising Him any further and denied His protection, a rather dismal prospect by our Christian standards. (See such passages as Job 7:9 f.; 16:22; Psalms 6:5; 30:9; 88:5, 10-12; 115:17; Isaiah 38:10-13, 18.)

There are scattered places in the Old Testament where men recognized the existence of life after death though such instances are few and rather obscure. Job 19:25 ff. is one such surge of belief and hope: "For I know that my Redeemer lives, and at last he will stand upon the earth; and after my skin has been thus destroyed, then from my flesh I shall see God, whom I shall see on my side, and my eyes shall behold, and not another." Psalm 23 hints of life after death when in closing it says, "Surely goodness and mercy shall follow me all the days of my life; and I shall dwell in the house of the Lord for ever" (v. 6).

Other quotes of interest include, "Thou dost

guide me with thy counsel, and afterward thou wilt receive me to glory" (Ps. 73:24), and "God will ransom my soul from the power of Sheol, for he will receive me" (Ps. 49:15).

Psalm 139:8 says, "If I ascend to heaven, thou art there! If I make my bed in Sheol, thou art there!" thus declaring that God as surely has access to Sheol as He does to heaven. Amos (9:2) uses a similar statement as a warning to the stubbornly disobedient, declaring that they cannot evade God's vengeance.

The faith that God is Lord even over death, though hesitant at first (1 Sam. 2:6), is affirmed ever more confidently (Hos. 6:2; 13:14) as Israel's experience progresses, until it is set forth comprehensively and positively in Daniel, the last book of the Old Testament to be written, "And many of those who sleep in the dust of the earth shall awake, some to everlasting life, and some to shame and everlasting contempt" (12:2).

It should be noted that resurrection was never an article of Jewish faith. In fact, it was possible to be a member in good standing in a Jewish congregation without holding any such belief. This is illustrated by the difference between the Pharisees, who believed in the resurrection, and the Sadducees, who did not, as pointed out in the New Testament (Mt. 22:23; Acts 23:8).

Much greater clarity on what lies beyond death comes with the teachings and life of Christ as recorded in the New Testament. Following Pentecost, faith in the resurrection is a major pillar of Christian doctrine. The Apostle Paul tells us that "if for this life only we have hoped in Christ, we are of all men most to be pitied" (1 Cor. 15:19).

An inseparable part of the good news which Christians proclaim is that for the followers of Christ death no longer needs to be feared. Its ultimate power has already been destroyed by the death and resurrection of Christ. This is the basis for Paul's crescendo of confidence, "For all things are yours, whether Paul or Apollos or Cephas or the world or life or death or the present or the future, all are yours; and you are Christ's; and Christ is God's" (1 Cor. 3:21-23).

Persons who lived before Christ could not gain a clear view of death until death was "beaten at its own game." But once death's grip was broken by Him who was life incarnate, the light began to dawn. Until Christ conquered death once for all, it had made slaves of all mankind, including God's people, as we have seen.

But now, if Christians believe what they profess to believe, death is drained of its domination and power. We may even taunt the former bully, whom we no longer have reason to fear, "O death, where is thy victory? O death, where is thy sting?" (1 Cor. 15:55). "Death is swallowed up in victory" (1 Cor. 15:54).

Tragically, death's grip continues to exercise its hold on much of mankind even though its stranglehold was broken almost 2,000 years ago. Partly, this is because Christians have not more faithfully and boldly proclaimed the gospel in every generation, and partly, it is because we have not fully grasped the significance ourselves of this part of the gospel.

21

Hebrews 2:14, 15 tells us, regarding Jesus' life and death, that He partook of the same human nature we have so that "through death he might destroy him who has the power of death, that is, the devil, and deliver all those who through fear of death were subject to lifelong bondage." The sting of death has been removed by the victory of Jesus. We who follow Him can live in a confidence and joy that the prospect of physical death does not daunt. Those who are alive when the Lord returns will be spared even this experience. In the meantime, all of us — Christian and non-Christian alike — will continue to experience the transition called death.

Let me share an idea concerning the phenomenon of physical death that I have been weighing for a long time. The prevalent Christian view is that physical death is the consequence of man's choosing to sin by disobeying the Lord. [4] Have you ever stopped to imagine what the outcome would have been had man not chosen to sin! Some plan for man's transition from this life to the next would have been necessary or planet earth would have had a population explosion like nothing we can even imagine!

Let me suggest for your consideration the possibility that physical death was a part of God's perfect plan from the beginning and that it has never been a penalty incurred as a result of disobedience. It is hard to conceive of God intending all those born on the earth to remain here for hundreds and thousands of years. Perhaps "translation" like that of Enoch and Elijah would have been an alternative, but death as a graduation or promotion from this life to the next may indeed have been God's wisdom from the beginning. This would suggest that it was *spiritual* death God spoke of when He warned Adam and Eve that *in the day* they ate the fruit of the forbidden tree they would die. He could hardly have meant physical death, for the Scriptures proceed to tell us that Adam lived to be 930 years old. The promptness of death promised them as the penalty of their disobedience must have referred to something other than physical death. The Bible tells us that "it is appointed for men to die once, and after that comes judgment" (Heb. 9:27), but this neither states nor implies that physical death is the consequence of sin, for indeed God has not appointed man to sin!

What the Apostle Paul says that bears on this interpretation is that "the sting of death is sin" (1 Cor. 15:56). He does *not* say, "The sting of sin is death," which is what we should expect were physical death the consequence of our sin. The inference rather may be that death would not have been a dreadful, threatening thing had man not sinned, even though physical death would have occurred just the same. However, since sin did enter, death took on a terrifying, vengeful aspect. Similarly Adam and Eve's attitude toward God changed after they sinned, though God sought them out for fellowship just as He had before. It was the first pair's own sense of guilt that prompted their hiding and distorted their attitude toward God from open, joyous, fellowship to dread and fear.

So fundamentally has our sinfulness skewed both our understanding of God's love and our ability to accept His love that even for Christians death still has remnants of dismay and grief. But the Apostle Paul, nevertheless, recognizes that Christians do not mourn as those do who have no hope. (See 1 Thessalonians 4:13.) The victory wrought by Christ over death on our behalf has removed the sense of dark finality that death would otherwise hold. Our Lord has brought the prince of devils to an unconditional surrender even though he continues to rage. Death is associated with sadness even for the Christian because of the trauma of separation. But death is no longer oppressive for Christians since we have the knowledge and assurance that it is the entry into Christ's presence which, as Paul said, "is far better." (See Philippians 1:21, 23.)

The Bible redefines the very word and idea which we call "death." It speaks of those outside of Christ as dead even while they live (1 Tim. 5:6) and of those who live "in Christ" as dead to sin but alive unto God (Rom. 6:11). There is a first death which is a death *to* sin brought about by our decision to accept Christ's forgiveness and walk in His word and will. For such people physical death is simply the means of our entry into the presence of the Lord. For the unbeliever the first death is their deadness *in* sin. The second death is the judgment which is to come with its horrors and separation from God "where their worm does not die, and the fire is not quenched" (Mk. 9:48). [5]

This is only a beginning, so far as the topic of death is concerned, but we are eager to move on to a discussion of life after death. What does the Bible have to tell us about the intermediate state between physical death and the ultimate resurrection of the just and the unjust? We shall turn to this now.

2

BETWEEN DEATH AND RESURRECTION

From a discussion of the transition we call death, we move to a consideration of the next stage of human existence which we shall call "the near hereafter" or "the intermediate life." By this we mean the period between death and the resurrection, the life we shall live after death but prior to the judgment.

In the first chapter we spoke of death as the termination of physical life for every human being, whether in reference to someone who has already made the transition or of us who have not yet passed this dramatic milestone in our existence.

In this chapter we will examine the second stage which none of us now reading these lines has yet experienced, but which all those who have lived and died since the dawn of creation are now experiencing — the near hereafter. We will join them in this intermediate life after our own deaths. Our discussion of "the far here-after" in later chapters will deal with the res-urrection, the judgment of all mankind, and the assigning of every human being to heaven or hell. This third and final stage has not yet arrived for anyone who has ever lived since the Creation.

It is commonly thought that at death people pass to their final destiny — heaven or hell. To the Christian such an idea is untenable since this would mean that persons would be summoned up for judgment after they have already spent perhaps thousands of years at their final destination! The Scripture seems to indicate that God does not assign any of the righteous or consign any of the wicked to their ultimate destinations until the time He will judge all men. Of the righteous, Hebrews 11:39, 40 tells us that all the heroes of faith mentioned in that great faith chapter, "though well attested by their faith, did not receive what was promised, since God had foreseen something better for us, that apart from us they should not be made perfect." As for the wicked, the Scriptures say they shall be sent to the place prepared for the devil and his angels. (See Matthew 25:41.) The words of Jude (v. 6) speak of this place as a temporary confinement even for the wicked angels: "And the angels that did not keep their own position but left their proper dwelling have been kept by him in eternal chains in the nether gloom until the judgment of the great day."

Our attitudes, acts, and decisions during life have already determined which of the two destinies we are bound for. Following death we go, as it were, to that waiting room outside the hall of final judgment. Judgment will not change our destiny but it will pronounce the sentence. It will so fully and fairly be tailored to each of our lives as to remove beyond all question any doubt we may have concerning the impartiality and fairness of God. Apparently at this time will also come that remarkable moment the Apostle Paul mentions in passing in 1 Corinthians 4:5. In admonishing us against pronouncing judgment prematurely, he instructs us to wait until the time when "the Lord comes, who will bring to light the things now hidden in darkness and will disclose the purposes of the heart. *Then every man will receive his commendation from God!*" (Emphasis mine.)

It is exceedingly difficult to describe briefly the Old Testament and rabbinical teachings about the near hereafter. The differing conceptions found interwoven through this literature are almost always vague, and sometimes contradictory. The Greek word "Hades" is the equivalent of the Hebrew word "Sheol," and the *Jewish Encyclopedia* tells us that Sheol "connotes the place where those that died were believed to be congregated. . . . Here the dead meet. . . without distinction of rank or condition — the rich and the poor, the pious and the wicked, the old and the young, the master and the slave — if the description in Job 3 [11-19] refers, as most likely it does, to Sheol. The dead continue after a fashion their earthly life. . . .Sheol is a horrible, dreary, dark, disorderly land (Job. 10:21,22); yet it is the appointed house for all the living.

. . . Return from Sheol is not expected (2 Sam. 12:23; Job. 7:9, 10). . . . It is described as man's eternal house (Eccles. 12:5)." [1] (Brackets mine.)

Christ gave His endorsement to the major lines of Jewish belief as held by the Pharisees. He used their phrases and words in speaking of life after death. He spoke of the rich man in Hades (not hell!) lifting up his eyes, being in torment, and of Lazarus being carried by the angels into Abraham's bosom — a reference to a particular section of Hades which was not horrible and dreary. (See Luke 16:22, 23.) Interestingly, the *Jewish Encyclopedia* cites Proverbs 7:27 and says that Hades "seems to have been viewed as divided into compartments." [2] Our Lord said to the repentant thief crucified beside Him, "Today you will be with me in Paradise" (Lk. 23:43). The *Jewish Encyclopedia* informs us that the word "Paradise" occurs but three times in the Old Testament (Song of Sol. 4:13; Eccles. 2:5; Neh. 2:8) and then comments: "In the apocalypses and in the Talmud the word is used of the Garden of Eden and its heavenly prototype. . . .From this usage it came to denote, as in the New Testament, the abode of the blessed (comp. Lk. 23:43; 2 Cor. 12:4; Rev. 2:7)." [3]

It is clear that our Lord did not mean the thief would join Him immediately in heaven, for He also said, "No one has ascended into heaven but he who descended from heaven, the Son of man" (Jn. 3:13). Even Jesus did not go at once to heaven when He died. He declared clearly at the time of His appearance to Mary Magdalene, "I have not yet ascended to the Father" (Jn. 20 :17). Where, then, did His spirit go after His burial and before His resurrection? From early times, the Apostles' Creed has included the phrase, "He was dead and buried, and descended into Hades. . . ." And Peter tells us in 1 Peter 3:19 and 4:6 that Christ's living spirit "went and preached to the spirits in prison . . . even to the dead." Peter declared in his sermon on the day of Pentecost that David "foresaw and spoke of the resurrection of the Christ, that he was not abandoned to Hades" (Acts 2:31).

This distinction concerning life between our earthly sojourn and our ultimate destiny was clearly taught by the early church. Paterson-Smyth quotes several of these church fathers on this point: Justin Martyr, AD 150, in his *Dialogue with Trypho* declared, "The souls of the godly abide in some better place and the souls of the unrighteous in a worse place, expecting the time of judgment. . . .Those who hold that when men die their souls are at once taken to heaven are not to be accounted Christians or even Jews." Irenaeus, AD 180, in *Against Heretics* said, "The souls of Christ's disciples go to the invisible place determined for them by God and there dwell awaiting the resurrection." Augustine, AD 354-430, commented, "During the interval between death and resurrection men's souls are kept . . . according as they severally deserve rest or punishment." [4] Could this be what our Lord alluded to when He said, "In my Father's house are many rooms" (Jn. 14:2)?

This whole teaching about the intermediate life has been obscured somewhat for those recent generations of Bible readers who have depended upon the King James Version. In this version the word "Hades" has been unfortunately translated "hell." In 1611 hell did not have the awful meaning it carries today. It was not used to refer to the lost. It simply meant what Hades and Sheol originally meant — the place of the dead without reference to whether they were righteous or wicked.

Heaven and hell (when used as the opposite of heaven) are always to be spoken of as states after the judgment. No one has ever yet gone to the ultimate heaven or hell. No one has yet been finally judged, much less damned. All who have ever died are waiting and will wait until all members of the human race that have ever lived are judged or rewarded at the same time.

The Bible does not tell us very much about the intermediate life. It is more concerned about being our guide in this life so that we shall be eligible for a blessed afterlife, both near and far. It concentrates on the urgency of people repenting of their sins, turning to Christ, accepting Him unconditionally as Savior and Lord, and walking steadfastly in His will as they grow in understanding and experience.

But, even so, more is revealed about this intermediate life than most Christians imagine. Only our Lord, who Himself experienced that strange land, has the ultimate wisdom to understand what we ought to know and what will profit us. Others who have returned from the dead (only to die again!) have contributed little or nothing to our understanding of life after death, probably because they could find no adequate words to describe their experience. (Needless to say, we cannot trust the efforts of spiritism to fill us in on the way it is "over there.")

Some Christians seem to think that there is something presumptuous in even inquiring into the mysteries of life beyond death. Such persons might even quote the verse in Deuteronomy 29:29, "The secret things belong to the Lord our God," as though the verse is saying in effect, "How dare you inquire about things which are not for you to know?" However, this is not the tone of this verse at all. The verse goes on to say, "But the things that are revealed belong to us and to our children for ever, that we may do all the words of this law." This seems to suggest that because we belong to God, we may expect to be let in on some family secrets! A reverent curiosity and an eagerness to know all that the Lord will reveal to us can only be pleasing to God. The Apostle Paul said to the Christians at Thessalonica, "We would not have you ignorant, brethren, concerning those who are asleep" (1 Thess. 4:13).

We do not want mere sentimentality and guesses. We do want what God chooses to reveal to us. If we draw some conclusions which we cannot definitely document from Scripture,

32

we do so only to the extent that they seem to be reasonable inference from what is said. We will need to be candid in distinguishing between what the Scripture says and what may only be inferred.

Acknowledgment must be given to the Scripture's use of the word "asleep" in reference to death. The belief that the soul sleeps between death and resurrection has been held sporadically in the church and is not necessarily considered heresy in the strictest sense due to the paucity of Scripture teaching on the intermediate state. The cause for this view rests mainly on three considerations: (a) that human existence demands the unity of body and soul and that therefore if the body ceases to function, so must the soul; (b) that Scripture's use of the term "sleep" for death is alleged to mean the cessation of consciousness; and (c) that consciousness between death and resurrection characterized by bliss or woe can not logically be experienced prior to the final judgment.

However, there is other biblical evidence that qualifies, if not refutes, the validity of this view. While the normal state of man is union of body and soul (and/or spirit), the possibility of a disembodied conscious existence is clearly suggested both by the fact that man is made in God's image and God is pure spirit and on the basis of such passages as Hebrews 12:23 and Revelation 6:9-11. As for the word "sleep" it may be used in a limited sense in reference to the physical body and to the cessation of any of the normal bodily functions. (See Matthew

27:52, John 11: 11-14, and Acts 13:36.) As for the third point above, to exclude the possibility of conscious bliss or woe from the intermediate state on the ground stated is also to rule out logically both the joyful assurance of salvation in this life and the foreboding of judgment to come, yet both are not only possible but common in human experience. See John 5:24, Philippians 1:23, 28 and 2 Corinthians 5:8.) [6]

Let us go to Christ the Source of our life. Just as He alone knows the questions of our hearts, so He alone knows the secrets of the world beyond death. He has given us some information and reassured us that we need not be afraid.

He does not tell us a great deal for the simple reason that we could not understand it if He would. We have neither the experience nor an adequate vocabulary to describe such a realm. The difficulty may be illustrated by the problem we would have attempting to describe the color green to a person blind from birth.

Our Lord drew the curtain back ever so little for us in His story of the rich man and Lazarus, as recorded in Luke 16:19-31. I have no intention of belaboring this point but I would emphasize that there are reasons for believing that this story is not a parable. In this case our Lord did not say, as He usually did when giving parables, that the hereafter is *like* so-and-so. Here He names one of the characters, which He generally did not do in His parables.

34

But even if it is a parable, it is told with un-usual directness and detail.

Clearly Christ is speaking of the near, and not the far, hereafter, for the men He mentions are not long dead. Indeed, the brothers of the rich man are still living. The rich man in Hades [5] is quite aware of that earthly life which he just left and which is continuing on the earth side by side with the life he is now living. This is the first lesson to be learned from this story. People "over there" are living a life unseen by us but parallel to our earthly existence.

Second, we notice that the life beyond is clearly a conscious life. Neither the rich man nor Lazarus nor Abraham are asleep or un-conscious but rather very much alive. They are thinking and speaking and feeling much as they did in their former life. The rich man's concerns reach back into his former life. He is eager that his five brothers be warned against living as he had and consequently coming to this place of torment. The rich man and Lazarus talk freely to one another even though a chasm has been fixed between them. The rich man is now showing more anxiety and evangelistic compassion concerning his brothers than he apparently ever had while living on earth with them.

Third, each person recognizes himself as the same individual he was while on earth and with the same basic attitudes except that both are more enlightened now. None of us will be someone different over there from what we are here. Even Jesus reassured His disciple Thomas on one of His reappearances after His resurrection by saying, "See my hands and my feet, that it is I myself" (Lk. 24:39). There is no break in memory or in any circumstance that characterized them in their earthly life. And the patriarch Abraham is able to converse with both of them. He says to the rich man, "Son, remember that you in your lifetime received your good things, and Lazarus in like manner evil things; but now he is comforted here, and you are in anguish" (Lk. 16:25).

Now isn't that exactly what you would have expected? It is all quite in accord with what the Scriptures teach us generally. A humble follower of Christ is, in the main, happy in the depths of his being even on the earth. He has an inner peace with God, in spite of many temporal troubles and distractions which he knows are only for the brief duration of his earthly life. All these are gone now, for he has passed out of the mists of earth into the fuller light of the eternal, where, as Paterson-Smyth says so aptly, "everything is seen at its full value, where money counts for nothing and love counts for everything." [6]

And conversely, the rich man (often called Dives) is tormented. For he, whatever his profession of faith, was in fact a godless man regardless of his religious affiliations and his philanthropic contributions. At his worst moments, when he was awake in the middle of the night and when his conscience spoke to him about the desperate needs around him, he was

36

momentarily tormented in his earthly life also. But because he was rich he had access to many distractions and could manage to a large extent to forget God. But now these sensual pleasures and distractions are gone. He had to leave his wealth back on the earth and now his poor soul stands naked and quaking before "the eyes of him with whom we have to do" (Heb. 4:13). Note that he is not in hell — that is a stage still to come. But our Lord tells us that already the rich man is in such torment that he would take extraordinary measures to warn his brothers if he could.

We ought not pass lightly over the expression "carried by the angels into Abraham's bosom" (Lk. 16:22). So precious was the memory of Abraham to the Jews that this phrase, "Abraham's bosom," spoke of an especially heartwarming prospect. (If anyone but Jesus had spoken of being carried by angels we would likely pass it over as a bit of poetic imagery. But Jesus had a lot to say about angels. He spoke of guardian angels for children and talked of the angels rejoicing over one sinner who repents.) I would suggest that here we have the Lord's authority for the ministry of angels in general and particularly at death — escorting those of us who are His in this life into the great and glorious land so utterly new and so completely indescribable to us prior to death. The rich man is allowed to face death alone, just as he had not depended on God in life. But Christ would not make one of His own endure the shock of glory without the companionship of a personal angelic escort. (You can call this sentimental drivel, if you like, but I cannot believe that Christ would speak so freely of angels if His references had no substance.)

Several other incidents in our Lord's life may yield some information on the intermediate life. In the Transfiguration (Lk 9:28-36) Jesus talked with Moses and Elijah. Evidently the two great souls, who long ago left this life, have all the while watched with intense interest the mighty scheme of redemption being worked out on earth. We can imagine the exultant joy that came to those in that afterlife when straight from the cross, Christ, the triumphant Victor, descended into Hades to proclaim the glad tidings to the dead! (See 1 Peter 3:19; 4:6.)

Another episode in the life of our Lord yielding a further testimony to the intermediate life is recorded in Matthew 22:23-33 (Mk. 12:18-27; Lk. 20:27-40). The Sadducees posed a rather ridiculous question in an attempt to embarrass Jesus for His support of the Pharisees' belief in the resurrection. Jesus countered the Sadducees by correcting their view at two points. They were ignorant of the Scriptures (even of the Pentateuch which was the only part they acknowledged to be authoritative) and furthermore they underestimated what God can do. Jesus did not respond in reference to the resurrection so much as to the intermediate life. Apparently in Jesus' view there is little point in a resurrection unless there is provision also for a continuing life for all between death and resurrection. He simply reminded them of God's statement in Exodus 3:6, "I am the God of your father, the God of Abraham, the God of Isaac, and the God of Jacob." Since all three patriarchs were long dead at the time God spoke these words, His use of "am" instead of "was" clearly infers their continuing conscious life even though separated from their physical bodies. Jesus adds the verbal thrust in summary, "He is not God of the dead, but of the living" (Mt. 22:32), thus endorsing a largely oral tradition of the Pharisees supported by only a smattering of Old Testament passages. Jesus did not base His confirmation of life beyond death on any partisan view but rather upon a passage well within the books which the Sadducees held to be trustworthy.

Another glimpse comes in connection with Jesus dying on the cross. In the very throes of death, our Lord responded with compassion to the plea of the thief dying beside Him. Jesus replied with assurance and precision, "Today you will be with me in Paradise" (Lk. 23:39-43). Note that the word our Lord used was Paradise, not heaven. Paradise is the resting place of good men after death (in contrast to Gehenna) and not a reference to the ultimate destiny to which all men will be assigned later. Our Lord assured the desperately fearful and dying thief of Christ's personal and conscious companionship in the afterlife. This implies mutual recognition of one another in the intermediate life.

The apostles and the Christians of the early centuries seem to have had a clearer understanding of our Lord's ministry during those days between His burial and resurrection than most Christians do today. Paul, in writing his Ephesian letter, speaks of the gifts which Christ bestowed on the church after His ascension. The word "ascended" prompts him to stop abruptly. He seems to fear that his readers will think that Christ's work was limited to that which He has accomplished since His ascension. Paul pauses to declare that Christ "also descended into the lower parts of the earth . . . that he might fill all things" (Eph. 4:9, 10). Paul wants us to know that just as in the future there shall come a day when "at the name of Jesus every knee should bow, in heaven and on earth and *under the earth*" (Phil. 2:10, emphasis mine), so prior to Christ's ascension Christ first proclaimed to those in the nether world the fact of His victory over every enemy. Let us not stumble at the apostle's use of spatial terms for what cannot be either confined or defined in such terms. Rather let us rejoice that he found any kind of words to convey to us the magnificence of our Lord's sovereignty.

A man by the name of St. Clement was born about fifty years after the Apostle John's death. Clement had a famous disciple named Origen who once encountered a famous infidel named Celsus. Celsus, knowing of the belief of the Christian church about Christ preaching in Hades, taunted: "I suppose your Master when He failed to persuade the living had to try to persuade the dead?" Whereupon Origen replied, "Whether it pleases Celsus or no, we of the church assert that the soul of our Lord, stript of its body, held converse with other souls, that He might convert those capable of instruction." [7]

Perhaps Christ's descent into Hades was the first great missionary effort of the Christian church, carried out by the Lord Himself since this realm was not accessible to His disciples! The Apostle Paul may have had a grander vision than we have imagined when he wrote, "For I am sure that neither death, nor life, nor angels, nor principalities, nor things present, nor things to come, nor powers, nor height, nor depth, nor anything else in all creation, will be able to separate us from the love of God in Christ Jesus our Lord" (Rom. 8:38, 39). Why is death mentioned first? The Scriptures tell us that "the last enemy to be destroyed is death" (1 Cor. 15:26). Paul began his cry of triumph by declaring that the most awesome and formidable enemy of all has indeed been vanquished!

3

MINISTRY AND GROWTH IN THE AFTERLIFE

"You have preached your last sermon," someone reminded Frederick Denison Maurice as he was dying.

"Yes," he replied, "the last sermon in *this* life."

The fact that this Church of England preacher/author/theologian believed he would continue preaching in the afterlife does not make it so, but the fact that he believed it is at least interesting. If continued meaningful activity lies ahead for Frederick Maurice, we can expect as much for ourselves.

We are committed in this book to the Holy Scripture. Wherever we venture to suggest anything beyond their explicit teaching, we do so with caution. We will try to proceed only as far as reasonable inference may permit. Since inference may be a matter of personal judgment, we do it with charity toward any who prefer not to indulge in inference or who believe that inference could lead in directions other than those suggested here.

In this chapter we are daring to probe the question, "Is the intermediate life one of purpose and function or is it only one of waiting until the end-time events?" We are focusing in this discussion only on those who have died "in Christ."

Both science and our own experience strongly lead us to believe that growth and change are universal laws of life. It seems evident that God's aim is not merely that we escape hell and get into heaven by the skin of our teeth. The Scriptures tell us God sent His Son to show us the way to mature personhood, "to the measure of the stature of the fulness of Christ," and to enable us by repentance and faith "to grow up in every way into him who is the head, into Christ" (Eph. 4:13, 15). The Scriptures are equally clear when they tell us that God is "of purer eyes than to behold evil" (Hab. 1:13), that even "the heavens are not clean in his sight" (Job 15:15), and that "nothing unclean shall enter it [the holy city], nor any one who practices abomination or falsehood, but only those who are written in the Lamb's book of life" (Rev. 21:27). The stakes are high but "God so loved the world that he gave his only Son, that whoever believes in him should not perish but have eternal life" (Jn. 3:16).

Since Christians are not perfected by the time death overtakes them, and since there is no entrance into that Holy City for any who are unclean, what hope is there even for Christians except that the necessary perfecting is accomplished in the near hereafter?

A major obstacle to our thinking on this topic is that we cannot think or speak of our future existence at all outside the time and space limitations of our earthly life. We have neither vocabulary nor powers of conception adequate for such an exercise. We proceed under these handicaps with the understanding that our projections could be more or less distorted. We are "going with what we've got."

Paul says in Philippians 1:6 that he is sure "that he who began a good work in you will bring it to completion at the day of Jesus Christ." Christ is seeing to our eventual perfection. We assume that this is being accomplished along the same lines as our present spiritual progress. [1] Our minds boggle when we attempt to understand *when* and *how rapidly* this will be accomplished in terms of time since we assume that the phrase "the day of Jesus Christ," refers to the end of time as we know it.

And what of those still living when Christ returns? First John 3:2 tells us that "it does not yet appear what we shall be, but we know that when he appears we shall be like him, for we shall see him as he is." This is the prospect for all of Christ's followers, regardless of whether they are living or dead at the time of His coming.

With whatever gradualness the progression toward perfection is accomplished in those who have entered the afterlife, it is possible that for those living when Christ returns the perfecting will be a speeded-up event. But for that vast number of godly persons who have died since the dawn of time, we presume in these pages that this perfecting process has been in operation ever since their decease. First John 3:2 implies that the perfection required of all who would enter into God's presence is not fulfilled in this life and consequently must be fulfilled in that life between death and resurrection. The following verse says that "every one who thus hopes in him purifies himself as he [Christ] is pure." Thus John acknowledges that growth in Christlikeness is a process which begins in this life and apparently extends into the next. It is not brought to completion until we see Christ as He is.

What is the nature of this growth in the afterlife? Is it a matter of personal advancement in Christlikeness, achieved by some isolated and individualized process of relationship and interaction with our Lord? Or is our growth a result of interrelationships with our Lord and with other maturing saints "over there" in much the same context that we Christians grew best in this life?

Occult spiritualism emphatically asserts not only the possibility of growth in the next life, and the ministry of souls there to one another, but holds that those in the afterlife are eager and able to minister to those still in this life. Ruth Montgomery reports that one of her spirit-contacts named Lily gave her a message in spirit-writing encouraging meditation as important because "it would make the crossover period that we call death less tedious, and would

45

permit a more accelerated advancement in the next plane. . . . You live on and on and on, but the time that is wasted in your soul's development can never be regained. . . . This is the ultimate goal toward which we all must strive, and the more rapid your progress there, the less time you will have to spend here in the tedious tasks that are essential to a soul's salvation. . . . We here on this side of the thin veil are less earth-bound than you, but still so near the earth that we must try to compensate for our faults in that life, and help others there before they come over. . . ." [2] Christians cannot, however, accept such counsel as anything but demonic in origin. We recall that the rich man's concern that someone warn his brothers was denied on the ground that they already had Moses and the prophets. This in addition to the explicit and stringent warnings against any resorting to spiritism. (See Deuteronomy 18:10-12 and Isaiah 8:19.)

Any growth in the afterlife would logically be related to ministry to others. God's call to Abraham was given in order that, as Abraham obeyed it, "all the families of the earth shall be blessed" (Gen. 12:3, alternate reading). God said, "I will make of you a great nation, and I will bless you, and make your name great, *so that you will be a blessing* (12:2, emphasis mine). In 1 Corinthians 12 to 14 Paul takes pains to explain that the gifts of the Spirit are for the benefit of the body above all! The principle is that in contributing to the good of others we ourselves "grow in the grace and knowledge of our Lord and Savior Jesus Christ" (2 Pet. 3:18). Paul says that as we utilize our God-given gifts and speak the truth in love we "grow up in every way into him who is the head, into Christ, from whom the whole body, joined and knit together by every joint with which it is supplied, when each part is working properly, *makes bodily growth* . . ." (Eph. 4:15, 16, emphasis mine).

Our Lord's preaching of the gospel to the dead (1 Pet. 4:6) was a ministry in the afterlife. Is it likely that our Lord would design such an intricate program of spiritual growth in this life for each of us by so many different means, and almost all of them of a reciprocal nature, and then abandon this entire process and substitute an utterly different one in the life hereafter? He could, to be sure, if in His sovereignty and wisdom He chose to do so, but with the evidence we have, it hardly seems likely.

Edersheim tells us, "The Rabbis . . . believed . . . that there were . . . seven departments in paradise, and as many in hell." [3] Commenting on the possibility of a multi-compartmentalized Paradise, Arthur Chambers proposes a fascinating line of thought. He writes, "There is such a thing as a '*babe* in Christ,' and a 'man in Christ.' If one enters that life [after death] as a babe in character and spiritual attainment, he must not expect that his lot, so long as he remains a 'babe,' will be cast among 'spirits made perfect.' There would be as much unfitness in it, as there would be in transplanting a child from an infant-school into a university, or in apportioning to a boy the environment of a man. St. Paul . . . was permitted an experience of the intermediate life of a very exalted kind, and he is very careful to describe his condition, at the time, as that of a 'man in Christ' (2 Cor. 12:2). Had he been a 'babe' when that experience was vouchsafed to him, his being caught up into Paradise,' would not have involved his entrance into 'the third heaven,' or sphere, of it.'' [4]

In our assumption that spiritual growth in the afterlife bears some resemblance to the process God has ordained for our growth in this life, it must also be assumed that time is not the factor it is here. This is beyond our comprehension, just as Peter's statement is, that "with the Lord one day is as a thousand years, and a thousand years as one day" (2 Pet. 3:8). The patriarchs who died in fullness of both age and faith thousands of years ago are neither being penalized or given an advantage by the delay of the return of Christ during the intervening millenniums. Neither the Christian who died in the first century AD nor the one who died last week has an unfair advantage or disadvantage. Time as we reckon it does not count after death.

It seems likely that the Holy Spirit continues with our sanctification in the next life at whatever point He was accomplishing His purpose in us at the time of our death. Those who have patiently and perseveringly advanced along the road of Christian growth for the greater part of a long earthly lifetime will surely find themselves appreciably nearer the goal in the next life than those whose life ends soon after choosing the Christian way. There is, of course, that troublesome parable of the husbandman who hired laborers at different hours of the day and paid them all the same amount (Mt. 20:1-16), but this is intended to teach us that anything we receive is a gift of God's mercy rather than a reward for our good works! We all are paid equally in the sense that we all go to be with Christ.

I once heard a person respond to a comment that a man had forty years' experience in a particular vocation: "No, Joe does not have forty years' experience," he said, "only one year's experience forty times over!" How sad! A similar situation prompted the apostles at times to rebuke their readers sternly for not progressing as they should have in their spiritual growth. In Hebrews 5:12 the author says, "For though by this time you ought to be teachers, you need some one to teach you again the first principles of God's word. You need milk, not solid food." The Apostle Paul is equally exercised in 1 Corinthians 3:1 when he laments, "But I, brethren, could not address you as spiritual men, but as men of the flesh, as babes in Christ." The Scriptures recognize no legitimate excuse for lack of spiritual growth once we have been born anew!

If indeed there is an intimate connection between our spiritual progress here and our experiences hereafter, how stupid it is for any of us to live a slipshod Christian life in the empty hope that, somehow or other, all will come out right in the afterlife! Yet one fears that this is too frequently the case with many Christians today! Why do so many professing Christians not give evidence of growth in grace? Why is there not more effort to rid themselves of defects in character? How can there be so many Christians who, despite all their church-going and orthodox beliefs, are nevertheless so unlovely, cold, and selfish? Intermingled with their orthodoxy, evidently, is the idea that their cultivation of Christlikeness is not a matter of paramount concern. They seem to assume rather that their adherence to certain doctrines and practices is all that is necessary.

Surely God means just what He says when we read that "whatever a man sows, *that* he will also reap" (Gal. 6:7, emphasis mine). This law applies just as certainly to a meager sowing of righteousness as it does to a sowing that is positively wicked! Small wonder that the Scripture contains such an air of urgency about our discipleship even to the extent that we are reminded in 1 Peter 4:17 that judgment must "begin with the household of God"!

The account of the rich man and Lazarus mentions a great gulf fixed between the two. This should not surprise us, since a similar gulf exists between the Christian and the unbeliever already in this life. Paul speaks of the utter inability of the carnal man to make any sense of the things of the Spirit (1 Cor. 2:14), and Peter speaks of those who are made to suffer for righteousness' sake (1 Pet. 3:14). It has been suggested that just as this gulf is not everlastingly fixed in this life, so it exists in the afterlife only so long as the dissimilarity continues. The preaching of the gospel by Christ to those who lived before the Flood (1 Pet. 3:18-20) is cited as evidence that our Lord crossed over that gulf. [5] We have no clear indication, however, that a similar crossover is possible for us. In fact, the dominant theme of the New Testament is the urgency both of our regeneration and of our progress in sanctification in this life. By what conceivable quirk of logic would anyone in his right mind choose to dawdle toward that perfection in Christ which is our ultimate destiny and our exquisite joy!

The Roman Catholic conception of purgatory is the end result of a line of thought which attempts to account for the questions we have been grappling with. This doctrine has been abhorrent to Protestants largely because of the abuses which were associated with it at the time of the Reformation in the early 1500s. Even the Roman Catholic conception deals only with those who will be ultimately saved. It offers no hope to those who enter the afterlife in an unregenerate state. The gross misuse and exploitation of the implications of this doctrine by an unscrupulous priesthood in the sixteenth century deserved the most vigorous repudiation. However, in all honesty, we must recognize that underlying those grotesque abuses are the very questions we have been considering.

God's plan for our redemption clearly involves a gradual unfolding of intermediate steps which began with God's call to Abraham or even earlier. The whole story of God and His people through the Old Testament and the New is an unfolding of His provision for men's salvation. And our individual salvation even as it is experienced in this life has its past, present, and future dimensions.

Paul tells us that God sent forth His Son "when the time had fully come" (Gal. 4:4). A major purpose of that divine life was not realized in history until our Lord cried out from the cross, "It is finished!" (Jn. 19:30). But even then He had a ministry to perform in relation to "the dead, that though judged in the flesh like men, they might live in the spirit like God" (1 Pet. 4:6). Christ's resurrection, His ascension, and the sending of the Holy Spirit on the day of Pentecost advanced other dimensions of His purpose and promised salvation.

Earlier in Christ's ministry we can observe other facets of His unfolding purpose in destroying the "works of the devil." When the seventy returned from their preaching and healing mission and reported with mingled surprise and joy that even the demons were subject to them in Christ's name, He replied, "I saw Satan fall like lightning from heaven" (Lk. 10:17, 18). Later, near the time of His crucifixion, the Lord declared, "Now is the judgment of this world, now shall the ruler of this world be cast out" (Jn. 12:31). But the final consignment of the enemy to his proper place of punishment and confinement is still future. This is evident from

Christ's account of the judgment when He shall say to those on his left, "Depart from me . . . into the eternal fire prepared for the devil and his angels" (Mt. 25:41).

We have only the meagerest hints of answers to the questions that come to our minds regarding the afterlife, whether for saints or sinners. Whether the wrath of God toward sin is eternally only redemptive or also punitive, we shall ultimately know that God has judged all mankind — every man, woman, and child who has ever lived, under any conditions — lovingly, fairly, impartially, for He is "not willing that any should perish" (2 Pet. 3:9, KJV). We do not know what process the infants who have left this life before maturing to full self-consciousness, or the mentally ill, or the severely retarded will go through in preparation for eternity with God. Perhaps we have a clue in Christ's own physical wounds which were not erased by His resurrection but rather were marks of identification and badges of victory! (See John 20:27, 28.) Wherever our loved ones may be, Christians shall be satisfied and their joy unqualified when once they go to be with Him, since our affections will not operate over there in the imperfect manner they do here. (See Matthew 22:30.) We shall know in the depths of our glorified beings that the Judge of all the earth had done right and we will experience neither sorrow nor regret.

We have endeavored to push what little information we have at our disposal concerning this topic as far as reverence and honesty with the Scripture will permit. We leave the topic with the conviction, accepted by faith, that it is best that we know only this much and no more. We shall leave any pursuit of more information from other channels to those willing to dabble in what the Scriptures tell us is sorcery and its related "arts" — a pastime that dooms the participants to "the lake that burns with fire and sulphur, which is the second death" (Rev. 21:8).

In closing, follow closely the words of a poem included in a book by A. H. Strong, a Baptist theologian, noting especially what he says concerning "their silent ministry":

I cannot think of them as dead
   Who walk with me no more:
Along the path of life I tread
   They have but gone before.
The Father's house has mansions fair,
   Beyond my vision dim;
All souls are His and, here or there,
   Are living unto Him.
And still their silent ministry
   Within my heart hath place;
As when on earth they walked with me
   And met me face to face.
Mine are they by an ownership
   Nor time nor death can free;
For God hath given to love, to keep
   Its own, eternally. [6]

4

THE COMMUNION
OF SAINTS

The phrase used as the title of this chapter is from the Apostles' Creed which dates from approximately the end of the fifth century AD. The communion of saints has come to refer to the fellowship between Christians in this life and those beyond death. Just when or where it was added, or its original meaning, are lost to obscurity. But the Apostles' Creed with this phrase intact has been generally accepted and continuously used by most Christian traditions, whether Roman Catholic or Protestant.

It is anyone's guess what meaning this phrase conveys today to the average Christian, but its presence in the creed seems not to stimulate controversy. If the simple meaning that a bond of fellowship unites believers on both sides of death represents a teaching or implication of the New Testament, we may continue to find the phrase useful in keeping a facet of our faith upon our minds and hearts. *The New Schaff-Herzog Religious Encyclopedia* states as at least a plausible theory that this "clause was originally put into the creed to express in the widest sense the fellowship of all the saints, existing already here and to be perfected hereafter." [1] It is in this sense that we are here considering its basis and import.

The phrase recognizes that in the New Testament the term "saint" refers to all followers of Christ and the word "communion" fundamentally means fellowship. It is an acknowledgment, in the first place, of the bond that unites all disciples to their common Lord, and second, that this bond is not severed by death. The Thessalonians feared that their fellow believers who had died would be denied a part in the resurrection. The Apostle Paul assured them on the authority of the Lord Himself that "we who are alive, who are left until the coming of the Lord, shall not precede those who have fallen asleep" in death (1 Thess. 4:15). He recognized that unity of believers in Christ is not broken even by the event of physical death.

Since ours is a living Lord and since Christians go to be with the Lord at the time of death, it is a striking and happy thought that He used the simile, "I am the vine, you are the branches" (Jn. 15:5). He was speaking of a reality that extends beyond the fellowship we enjoy with Him and one another in this life. It is appropriate that the Episcopal communion service explicitly recognizes that the same functions of His body continue "there" that we are accustomed to here — namely praise and worship. It is not we in this life alone who find Christ the center of our praise and service. Our fellow believers in the life beyond also focus their attention upon Him — perhaps far more perfectly there than we can here! Paterson-Smyth expresses his excitement thus: "Why, we could do everything for each other that we can do on earth when separated by the Atlantic — except just write home. . . . We are very close if we would but realize it.

> "Death hides, but it does not divide
> Thou art but on Christ's other side;
> Thou art with Christ and Christ with me,
> In Him I still am close to thee." [2]

You may be thinking, "Yes, that's a beautiful thought but is that all? Do those who have gone on before know or care about my joys and sadnesses? Even if they are living a conscious life, are they concerned about us? Or are they completely cut off from any awareness, much less concern, about life here?" Let us review some Scriptures that provide a few hints in answer to our questions.

In the story of the rich man and Lazarus, Abraham answered the rich man's plea that Lazarus be sent to warn his brothers, "They have Moses and the prophets; let them hear them" (Lk. 16:29). Abraham is speaking of other servants of God who came a thousand years after his own time on earth, yet he is well informed of those subsequent persons. The rich man argues that an extraordinary visit would persuade the brothers. Abraham answers categorically that if they have not responded to the message of the Lord's own prophets, they would not respond even though someone would rise from the dead. How aptly this reply speaks to spiritualism's major appeal today, that living men need communication with those beyond death. The history of spiritualism certainly does not bear out the contention that people grow in godliness best if only they can hear from those beyond death.

Another passage significant for its rich implications is found in John 8:56 following the Jews' harassment of Jesus with their unbelief and scorn. Jesus replied, "Your father Abraham rejoiced that he was to see my day; he saw it and was glad." This matter-of-fact report from the afterworld seems to speak both to the attitude of Abraham prior to Christ's incarnation and afterward! Jesus was possibly in touch with the "other side" even after His incarnation so that He was able to report Abraham's present reaction to His own ministry which was then in progress.

A third passage pertinent here even though we have already discussed it in another connection is the account of Christ's Transfiguration as recorded in Luke 9; Matthew 17; and Mark 9. On this occasion Moses and Elijah "materialized" from the invisibility of the intermediate life to speak with Jesus concerning His death. Unless we are ready to say that the righteous on the other side have interest only in Christ, this is a strong hint of their keen awareness of life on earth and their watchful participation in our affairs.

Perhaps the most striking passage of all is the opening verse of Hebrews 12. Even though the word translated "witnesses" is the word "martyrs" and not the word meaning "spectators," most commentators are inclined to believe that there is here the thought of spectators in an amphitheater watching a race. William Barclay sees "witnesses" used in a double sense, "for they are those who have witnessed their confession to Christ and they are now those who are witnesses of our performance. . . . It is of the very essence of life that life is lived in the gaze of the heroes of the faith who lived and suffered and died in their day and generation. How can a man avoid the struggle for greatness with an audience like that looking down upon him?" [3]

John Wick Bowman says, "The author thinks of the ancient heroes of faith as a great 'cloud of witnesses' surrounding the contemporary generation of the Christian community. His words suggest that he has in mind the spectators in an amphitheater viewing the athletic games of the day, or those who have already run their part of the race." [4]

Charles A. Trentham comments, "Performers are often inspired when great athletes of former days are known to be in the stands observing them. . . .The young church was running that race, and what the saints of old once saw in the future is now taking place in the present, and they are now looking on as actual spectators.

Their faith would be fulfilled now as they witness the final triumph of the people of God"[5] in order, as the writer of Hebrews says, "that apart from us they should not be made perfect" (Heb. 11:40)!

Someone may say, "How could they be happy if they see the imperfections of our obedience?" But the question is, "What is 'better' as Paul said, about being with the Lord in the intermediate life if it promises only a peaceful contentment like that of a cow that forgets her young?" Our experience in this life is that the more Christlike we grow, the more sorrow we feel for the condition of others. Christ Himself has more sorrow than anyone else for the sins and troubles of men. There are surely higher things in God's plans for His saints than self-centered happiness and contentment. There is the blessedness that comes through sympathy with Him over human sorrow and pain. We degrade the thought of the blessedness of the redeemed when we suppose that they are less sensitive in the next life than they were in this one.

If, as our Lord said, there is joy in heaven over one sinner who repents (Lk. 15:7) does this not imply that there is pain in God's presence throughout this time of grace over those who do not repent? This may change after the end-time events have transpired. With the occurrence of those cataclysmic events a whole new chapter will be initiated that is quite beyond our concern at this time. If there are different ages, as the Scriptures clearly suggest, then we must not assume that the distant future will be nothing more than a refinement and continuation of the present.

From the centuries immediately following the death of the last apostle have come many explicit writings concerning the advisability of Christians on both sides of death praying for (not "to"!) one another. This concept has in its favor the thought that a communion of the saints would normally be expected to be a mutual benefit flowing both ways. But most of us shrink from this idea. We recognize that there are doctrines and concepts which appear very early in Christian history but which we choose nevertheless to reject — unless, indeed, we are ready to espouse the Catholic concept and put tradition on relatively equal par with Holy Scripture. We are not ready to do this even though we are at times in this book giving some ever so tentative consideration to inferences made explicit only by later tradition.

We will close this brief treatment of the communion of saints with a final daring illustration taken from the testimony of a contemporary that seems to bear marks of Christian authenticity. This experience of J. B. Phillips, the well-known and much beloved Episcopalian clergyman, author, and translator of the New Testament, is recorded in his book *Ring of Truth:* "Many of us who believe in what is technically known as the Communion of Saints must have experienced the sense of nearness, for a fairly short time, of those whom we love soon after they have died. This has certainly happened to me several times. But the late C. S. Lewis, whom I did not know very well and had only seen in the flesh once, but with whom I had corresponded a fair amount, gave me an unusual experience. A few days after his death, while I was watching television, he 'appeared' sitting in a chair within a few feet of me, and spoke a few words which were particularly relevant to the difficult circumstances through which I was passing. He was ruddier in complexion than ever, grinning all over his face and, as the old-fashioned saying has it, positively glowing with health. The interesting thing to me was that I had not been thinking about him at all. I was neither alarmed nor surprised nor, to satisfy the Bishop of Woolwich, did I look up to see the hole in the ceiling that he might have made on arrival! He was just *there* — 'large as life and twice as natural.' A week later, this time when I was in bed, reading before going to sleep, he appeared again, even more rosily radiant than before, and repeated to me the same message, which was very important to me at the time." [6]

There is little indeed in this account that is even remotely comparable to a spiritualistic seance — whether in expectation, context, or the need for a medium! There is almost nothing here that would prompt one to do anything but contrast this experience with the strange pursuits of that other Episcopalian clergyman, the late Bishop Pike! Furthermore, Phillips' embarrassment with another of his fellow clergymen, John Robinson, is evident in this recounting of his experience!

Perhaps the relative rarity of such experiences among Christians (though these things probably happen more than most of us imagine!) is but an indication of the privacy with which God, in His wisdom, sends such experiences into the lives of His people. It may be that one of the things that makes the occult so abhorrent in God's sight is its utter selfishness and arrogance in usurping His throne and renouncing a life of faith in order to get on with our own agenda, by fair means or foul! Is this not the pride that brought man's downfall in the Garden of Eden! Will we not be content with what God wishes to provide us in terms of information concerning the hereafter? Can we not rest in the confidence that our Lord will not deny us any good thing?

5

WHAT IS THE
RESURRECTION?

Robert Flockart lived and worked in the city of Edinburgh, Scotland, about a hundred years ago. He was not an ordained minister but he was a well-known character who proclaimed the gospel in the open air every night for more than 45 years! While speaking one night on being "put to death for our trespasses and raised for our justification" (Rom. 4:25) he told the following stories to illustrate his message:

"An aunt of mine died and left me a large sum of money in her will, but the will was contested by relatives, and I received nothing.

"On another occasion an ex-Sunday school pupil of mine who had rejected the gospel, and who was under sentence of death, invited me to come to his cell and pray with him. With tears in his eyes, he said, 'Mr. Flockart, you are the best friend I have on earth, and I am leaving to you all my possessions.' However, the young man did not die, since he received a pardon. I received nothing again.

"But now, dear friends, I want to tell you a

far greater story. The best Friend I ever had, the Lord Jesus Christ, the Son of God, died for me on the cross of Calvary, and willed to me eternal life. And, praise the Lord, on the third day, he rose again to make sure I got it!'' [1]

Flockart reflected a sound Christian conviction. Christ's rising again in the body on the third day was itself the capstone of the eternal life which He promised to His followers. It is not Christ's teachings, nor His miracles, nor His crucifixion, *but His resurrection* that is the apex of Christian doctrine!

One need only read the article on "Resurrection" in the *Jewish Encyclopedia* to see with what ambivalence and variety of definition this concept has been treated. The concept of immortality is found among all the great world religions, past and present, with a considerably greater degree of similarity in conception and elaboration than can be found when the claim is made that both body and spirit are to live on. It is precisely at this point that Christian doctrine is unique. No other founder and chief prophet offers himself (and this within recent historical time) as an exhibit of what the promised body will be like. All the statements of other religions concerning existence beyond this time are made without providing a living proof of the future prospect, not to mention the presence and frequent appearance of that proof-sample over a period of forty days between Christ's resurrection and ascension. The older Hebrew conception of life regarded the nation so entirely as a unit that no individual

65

mortality or immortality was considered. [2]

It is possible that the idea of resurrection does not originate with Christianity, or even Judaism. But so far as the history of religions has been able to trace, only Christianity has the audacity to make resurrection the keystone of its entire structure. The Apostle Paul penetrated deeply into the rationale of the Christian faith when he was led to say unequivocally, "If for this life only we have hoped in Christ, we are of all men most to be pitied" (1 Cor. 15:19). And he said this in the midst of his fullest exposition of bodily resurrection.

Even the Jewish development of the concept of resurrection could not finally rest with including it as an article of faith. The *Jewish Encyclopedia* article concludes: "In modern times the belief in resurrection has been greatly shaken by natural philosophy, and the question has been raised by the Reform rabbis and in rabbinical conferences whether the old liturgical formulas expressing the belief in resurrection should not be so changed as to give clear expression to the hope of immortality of the soul instead. This was done in all the American Reform prayerbooks. At the rabbinical conference held at Philadelphia it was expressly declared that the belief in resurrection of the body has no foundation in Judaism, and that the belief in the immortality of the soul should take its place in the liturgy."[3]

Even regarding belief in the immortality of the soul, man proceeds on uncertain footing. Thomas Babington Macaulay put it quite tersely when he wrote, "All the philosophers, ancient and modern, who have attempted without the help of revelation to prove the immortality of man, from Plato down to Franklin, appear to us to have failed deplorably." [4] Arthur H. Compton sums it up from the scientific and technological standpoint: "Science cannot supply a definite answer to this question. Immortality relates to an aspect of life which is not physical, that is, which cannot be detected and measured by an instrument, and to which the application of the laws of science can at best be only a well-considered guess." [5]

Both the idea and the doctrine of the resurrection surfaces in the life and teachings of our Lord in a way that is fuller, fresher, and more forceful than at any other time in history. Whatever the rich legacies of the great thinkers and cultures of the ancient past, they have left no contribution to the concept of the resurrection of the body worthy to be compared with the teaching and example of Christ. When we say in the Apostles' Creed, "I believe in Jesus Christ. . . who . . . the third day arose from the dead," and, "I believe in . . . the resurrection of the body," we are confessing something which no other world religion has effectively included in its creed and doctrine. (At the best some do affirm a return to life but none offers more than mythological evidence for it.)

It is precisely the differences that resurrection represents over any concept of immortality that are the uniquely new factors in the New Testament accounts and in Christianity over any other religion. Concern for the survival of human personality and values beyond death is not at all a new departure — practically every religion has spoken to this concern in some way. Ray Summers is quite correct when he says, "Any view of future survival which leaves out this restoration of the body from death back to life cannot be spoken of as a resurrection in the New Testament meaning of the term." [6]

The Apostle Paul boldly says that unless the resurrection of the body is true as exemplified by Christ, then our Christian faith is in vain and we are still in our sins! (See 1 Corinthians 15:16, 17.) This is tantamount to saying that unless resurrection is true, we are no better off than before. The Scriptures make it abundantly clear that more hinges on the resurrection than upon any other single Christian belief.

Wilbur M. Smith comments, "When such an impartial work as the *Oxford English Dictionary* wholly ignores Osiris rituals, Greek myths, and Zoroastrian speculation, and gives as the first definition of the word resurrection, 'the rising again of Christ after His death and burial,' it bears witness to the uniqueness of this event in world history." [7] Arnold Toynbee in his epochal *Study of History* lists 87 events and aspects of the life of Christ for which he says parallels can be found in the stories of the heroes of antiquity. But it is significant to note that there is no event in the ancient world that is worthy of being placed alongside the New

Testament account of Christ's resurrection. [8]

The disciples puzzled particularly over Christ's prediction of His own rising from the dead as they descended the Mount of Transfiguration. (See Mark 9:10.) Christ had already spoken of His resurrection in connection with His first cleansing of the temple when He responded to the Jews' request for a sign of His authority with the words, "Destroy this temple, and in three days I will raise it up" (Jn. 2:19). The account proceeds to tell us that it was only after Jesus was in fact raised from the dead that the disciples remembered His prediction and believed what He said. If we have difficulty believing in the resurrection, we may at least take comfort in the fact that Christ's own Twelve struggled with the same doubts.

It was the preaching of this doctrine that "turned the world upside down," according to the lament of Paul's enemies. (See Acts 17:3, 6.) The sermon preached to the crowd in response to the events of the day of Pentecost when the Holy Spirit came upon the disciples was a challenge built upon the prophetic Scriptures, the empty tomb, and the risen Lord, declaring that God had made this Jesus, whom the Jews had crucified, both Lord and Christ. (See Acts 2.) Paul repeatedly was called upon to defend the resurrection before the rulers of his day. (See Acts 24:21, for example.)

The contemporaries of the apostles shared many of the same difficulties people still have with the idea of resurrection. Of all that was new and different in Paul's message to the philosophers on Mars' Hill, it was specifically "when they heard of the resurrection of the dead [that] . . . some mocked" (Acts 17:32). And Paul in his epistle to the Christians at Corinth mentioned that some of them were saying, "There is no resurrection of the dead" (1 Cor. 15:12). He advised Timothy to avoid the godless chatter of such people as Hymenaeus and Philetus, "who have swerved from the truth by holding that the resurrection is past already" (2 Tim. 2:16-18). These distortions were all current in apostolic times beside the rejection of the concept by the Sadducees encountered during Christ's earthly life.

A remarkable variety of theories have been proposed as explanations and interpretations of the doctrine of the resurrection of Christ. This is a left-handed indication of its supreme importance. The more crucial a doctrine is to the whole structure of a faith, the greater the attempt will be by the enemies of that faith to discredit it. Let's look briefly at a number of these theories:

(1) *The stolen body theory* is of course the oldest. It was advocated by the chief priests and the elders as the story to be used by the guards when explaining why Jesus' body could not be found. (See Matthew 28:11-15.)

(2) *The swoon theory* holds that Jesus was not dead when buried. He simply revived when His body came into contact with the cool tomb and the odor of the spices.

(3) *The wrong tomb theory* proposes that the women who went early to what they believed

70

was the Lord's tomb met a young man there whom they mistook for an angel. This man, in an attempt to help them, told them they were looking at the wrong place and that another tomb had been used. The women misunderstood him and reported instead that an unused tomb had been Christ's.

(4) *The vision theory* dares, against all New Testament evidence, to suggest that the disciples believed so firmly that Jesus would be raised that they had visions or hallucinations to confirm their expectations and either didn't know or didn't admit the difference!

(5) *The television theory* holds that the ascended Lord sent back pictures of Himself in bodily form and that these convinced the disciples that they had indeed seen Him. (Imagine Thomas, the sturdy skeptic, being persuaded of the reality of the resurrection by placing his hands in the pictured wound-prints of the Lord!)

(6) *The legendary theory* suggests that the attempts of the early believers to account for Jesus' impact upon them developed into the myth of His return in the flesh.

(7) *The hyperbolic theory* says that Christ's disciples used such strong language to describe His continuing life among them that they were understood to be speaking literally.

(8) *The annihilation theory* holds that God disposed of Jesus' body so that only a spiritual nature could be understood to survive death. This is a theory similar to the Old Testament account of God's burial of Moses.

For most Christians, the above alternatives are harder to believe than to accept the New Testament accounts at face value. The resurrection of Christ holds for the Apostle Paul a corollary regarding all of us. If Christ has in fact been raised, then resurrection is certain for every human being, righteous or wicked. Not only our spirits will be immortal, but also our bodies. Together they constitute our person and God has chosen to provide for our preservation as a whole person rather than as a spirit only. It is not as though the inner you alone is the real you and that your body is dispensable! No, even though the bodies of the saints are to be "glorified," yet they will be recognizable and will manifest many of the same characteristics then that they do now.

Any suggestion that our bodies are to be thought of as a hindrance, an unnecessary wrapper, a limiting handicap as so many religions, ancient and modern, have seemed to suggest, is by the resurrection pronounced erroneous. Our bodies are not nuisances that can be shed to our benefit, nor obstacles to our spirit's freedom. Quite the contrary, our bodies are an essential aspect of our very being. While the desires of our flesh may be spoken of as carnal by nature, yet the glorification of the human body which Christ provides will correct that situation also. Even the temporary separation of our spirits and bodies from death until the resurrection is a matter of concern. While this is a part of God's plan, it is a condition that awaits correction at the resurrection when they will be joined together again. "For while we are still in this tent, we sigh with anxiety; not that we would be unclothed, but that we would be further clothed, so that what is mortal may be swallowed up by life" (2 Cor. 5:4).

The Scriptures nowhere speak disparagingly of the body. Christianity honors the body. God has been pleased to make it the temple of the Holy Spirit during this age. The body has been supremely honored by the incarnation of the Son of God. God, we are told in Jude 9, did not allow the devil to get possession of the body of Moses though Satan contended mightily for it.

The very idea of resurrection was so difficult for the disciples to conceive of that it is small wonder they saw Jesus' familiar figure following His death but did not recognize Him. They undoubtedly expected more obvious differences between an ordinary body and a resurrected body than what they saw in the appearances of the resurrected Lord. This probably accounts for the fact that those walking from Jerusalem to Emmaus did not recognize Jesus at first, even though they knew Him well and were grieving over His death. (See Luke 24:13-16.) They had simply dismissed from their minds any possibility of His return to a life such as they knew.

Martha in the death of Lazarus episode acknowledged a belief in her brother's resurrection at the last day (Jn. 11:24), but could not imagine his immediate return to life. Those disciples by the lake also "did not know that

73

it was Jesus" (Jn. 21:4). Mary, in the garden where Jesus was buried, mistook Jesus for the gardener (Jn. 20:15).

The point in all these instances is that even the followers of Jesus did not really expect a resurrected person to look, seem, feel, and act so much like that same human being did prior to death. They mistook Jesus not because He was so changed but because they did not imagine that a resurrected person would be so identical to that person's former appearance. Either they did not recognize Him or doubted His reality. Jesus had to reassure even His closest disciple on one occasion, "A spirit has not flesh and bones as you see that I have" (Lk. 24:39). He ate fish before them (Lk. 24: 41-43) as further evidence of the material reality of His presence. All of these instances argue for the substantial similarity in all respects of the resurrected Jesus and His former physical presence.

The resurrected body is, nevertheless, utterly different in some respects. It is a spiritual body, Paul says in 1 Corinthians 15:44, and as such is imperishable, powerful, glorified. For Paul to speak of a "spiritual body" is a contradiction in terms as these terms are generally used. But in speaking of the resurrection, we must use words in unconventional ways. Christ passed through the graveclothes leaving them undisturbed except that they no longer contained anything! He was capable of passing through the stone at the tomb's entrance and through the closed door of the room where the disciples were gathered. He was fully recognizable even to his most skeptical disciple, Thomas. He was able to vanish instantly, or gradually, as when He ascended into a cloud. (See John 20; 19, 26-29 and Acts 1:9.)

What will be the exact order of end-time events? Will it be resurrection/judgment/return of Christ, or return of Christ/judgment/resurrection, or perhaps some other sequence, such as judgment/resurrection/return of Christ? We cannot be sure. What is more important is that these are all closely associated with one another. While we experience something of the resurrection life here and now — those who refuse Him are condemned already (Jn. 3:18) — yet this partial realization of their significance does not exclude their future, fuller, and final consummation.

I cannot think of a better way to conclude this chapter than with the words of the Lord found in John 5:25-29:

Truly, truly, I say to you, the hour is coming, and now is, when the dead will hear the voice of the Son of God, and those who hear will live. For as the Father has life in himself, so he has granted the Son also to have life in himself, and has given him authority to execute judgment, because he is the Son of man. Do not marvel at this; for the hour is coming when all who are in the tombs will hear his voice and come forth, those who have done good, to the resurrection of life, and those who have done evil, to the resurrection of judgment.

6

THE RETURN
OF CHRIST

The event we wish to examine in this chapter is variously referred to as Christ's return, the second coming, the Parousia, and the second advent. The first coming of Jesus possessed a unique significance. It marked the entrance into the world of a moral force and a spiritual guide altogether unparalleled in the religious progress of mankind. As the Son of God, who revealed and represented God in His own person and whose mission it was to redeem men from sin, Jesus came to prove Himself in the truest sense to be the Messiah whom the Jewish people had long been expecting. Though He came to an ancient and proud race, His ethnicity has not frustrated, either in His own lifetime nor in the centuries since, God's purpose that He be "a light for revelation to the Gentiles, and for glory to thy people Israel" (Lk. 2:32).

Though He appeared in the world to found the kingdom of God in its true spiritual meaning, Jesus repeatedly intimated that the object of

His mission would not be perfectly attained in His first coming among men. There was to be a break in His visible connection with earthly affairs (Mt. 16:21); He would depart for a time (Jn. 14:19; 16:7); but He promised that He would come again to continue His work and carry it on to complete fulfillment. In fact, as the clouds of danger closed in on His earthly ministry, and a violent death loomed in view, He began to speak with growing frequency of a marvelous and triumphant return, in which His living presence and power would be gloriously revealed.

His sayings on this subject are not easy to interpret and they do not all refer to the same event. It is not that He spoke of His return sometimes in clear and sometimes in cryptic language, but that whenever He spoke of it He spoke enigmatically. There must have been reasons for this persistent ambiguity, not the least of which have been the spiritual dullness of His disciples and their unpreparedness for clearer teaching. For when the expectations are as erroneously and politically fixed as they were for the apostles, so that on the eve of Christ's ascension they were still asking, "Will you at this time restore the kingdom to Israel?" (Acts 1:6), one is not surprised to find Jesus saying to His followers, "I have yet many things to say to you, but you cannot bear them now" (Jn. 16:12).

The Lord was content to prepare them for the following facts:

(1) That He was about to leave them.

77

(2) That His death would result from His rejection by the hierarchy and the antagonism of the populace.

(3) That the sin of that generation which culminated in His death would speedily receive its punishment in the utter destruction of Jerusalem and the temple.

(4) That He Himself would, by His spiritual might, be the just avenger on Jerusalem of His own death.

(5) That an unspecified length of time would then follow during which the gospel would be preached throughout the world and the curse on the Holy City would last until the times of the Gentiles are fulfilled.

(6) That not until the whole world was evangelized would He visibly appear again.

(7) That, in the meantime, He Himself though visibly withdrawn, would be spiritually present with them and succeeding generations.

It was too much to expect that these facts, so plain to us, could have been grasped by those who, having found the Messiah, expected immediate victory at His hands. Their spiritual dullness and misunderstanding of Christ's program even after forty days of post-resurrection instruction are evident. In light of this, we may be quite certain that during the days spent with Him prior to His death and resurrection, they would have been absolutely unable to understand Him had He spoken openly of His continuous spiritual presence, of His judgment of Jerusalem during their lifetime, and of the many centuries of the gospel dispensation which were to pass before His final visible return. But what He could do, He did in words that hiddenly contained these truths. He revealed them enigmatically. The logic of events and the coming of the Spirit would interpret them to His hearers and to the church after them. The entire chapter of John 16 constitutes an attempt by Jesus to explain this process to His disciples to alleviate their fears, speak to their perplexities, and reassure them that He would not orphan or abandon them in any sense.

This diligent attempt to prepare His disciples with such earnest assurances as they were capable of receiving in their utter sorrow and confusion accounts in large measure for the ease with which the early church changed her views regarding the time of His return. Though they could scarcely accept it, He insisted that it was to their advantage that He go away (Jn. 16:7). He told them that the Spirit would instruct them fully in due time, and that the Spirit would do so only upon Christ's explicit authority (16:15). At first the fledgling church lived in expectation of an immediate return of her Lord. When years passed and subsequent events proved that this hope was illusory, the church proved able, without any great rupture of faith, to accept the view that a period of unknown length would intervene before Christ returned in His glory.

This revolution of thought can best be accounted for by the fact that when He did not come back with any such immediacy as they expected, they turned again to His words. They learned by the direction of the Holy Spirit and by what the circumstances now made plain, the deeper and truer meaning of His pregnant sayings.

So it is that we are still learning what the Lord means when He says, "I will come again and will take you to myself" (Jn. 14:3). His meaning cannot be exhausted by understanding His words to refer to Pentecost, or to death, or the Parousia, though His words include all these meanings in a profound manner. Similarly, His word "I will not leave you desolate; I will come to you" (14:18) is not sufficiently interpreted by understanding the words to refer only to the resurrection, or Pentecost, or to a personal spiritual witness to our own spirit, but must rather include all these. In both these verses the Greek tense is not future but present, meaning not "I will come" but "I come; at all times I am coming." Yet this view of repeated comings in various senses does not prevent John from teaching the great and final coming as well.[1]

In the preceding chapter we closed by saying we were not concerning ourselves with the order of the end-time events of resurrection, judgment, and Parousia, since it was the significance of these events to our general topic that was pertinent and not the technical order of them. To this we still subscribe but we will venture now to state a preference, however tentatively, for the purpose of this and the next several chapters in this study.

It seems that the Parousia will be the signal for the resurrection of the dead, both bad and good, just as those verses of John 5:28, 29 (quoted in closing the previous chapter) seem to suggest, and that the resurrection will then be followed by the judgment of mankind. The hearing of "the voice of the Son of God," which Christ speaks of (v. 25), seems to describe the same event as Paul comments on when he says, "For the Lord himself will descend from heaven with a cry of command. . . . And the dead in Christ will rise . . ." (1 Thess. 4:16). The hearing of Christ's voice is a euphemism for Christ's literal, visible return.

It is not easy to lay aside an assumption of Christ's early return and replace it with another view. It is hard for most of us to admit we were wrong and the new viewpoint delays the realization of a longed-for event. The early church did succeed in making this adjustment concerning the imminence of the Lord's return. But misunderstandings regarding Christ's return have recurred over and over through the centuries. The Scriptures need to be studied again and again if the Christians of any generation, with one set of impressions, are to be corrected and their feet set upon a better understanding. A patchwork quilt of texts may be put together in an ever so appealing and seemingly scriptural manner (as, for example, the Scofield Bible notes) but the passing of the years will require constant revisions and reconstructions to be relevant. We must repeatedly return to the New Testament to check our bearing again.

Evidence scattered down through Christian history suggests that some disciples in every era tend to think along the same lines that prompted the disciples to ask the Lord prior to His ascension, "Lord, will you at this time restore the kingdom to Israel?" (Acts 1:6). Luke says of the days prior to Christ's first Advent that "the people were in expectation" (3:15). When times are hard, the unrighteous are prospering, and wickedness flourishes, an irrepressible longing develops for release from bondage and a recovery of justice and mercy. It is small wonder then that in eagerness for light and hope Christians turn to the Scriptures and under special circumstances believe they find a tangible hope to which they may zealously give themselves. Obviously the disciples' preconceptions had not been uprooted by the time of the ascension or they would not have persisted in asking a question which Christ had earnestly tried to respond to on numerous occasions before. What Christ's teachings failed to do, however, subsequent events did accomplish. This process will undoubtedly continue to run its cycle again and again until Christ does in fact return and wrap up human history.

So corrupt and chaotic were conditions in Europe in the early 1500s that the expectation of the imminence of the second coming was not uncommon among the Reformers. The Reformation triggered by Martin Luther was interpreted by many as the major sign of the end of the world. Bernhard Rothmann, an Anabaptist theologian of Westphalia, Germany, reasoned, as sometimes Luther himself did, that the Reformation's recovery of the gospel after many centuries of eclipse must point to the nearness of the second coming. On the basis of this conviction Rothmann turned to Scripture and contrived a speculative numerology that reinforced his certainty of the imminence of Christ's return. He began by citing the case of the prophet Elijah who foretold the future, proclaimed God's Word, and was deterred by some hundreds of false prophets.

Now follow his line of thought carefully: Elijah prayed for the punishment of the sin, and the nation was struck with drought and trouble for 3 1/2 years. (See 1 Kings 18:1; Luke 4:25; and James 5:17.) Accordingly, 3 1/2 years is the simple punishment of those who were led astray and scornfully made light of God's Word. Indeed, the Bible commonly sets forth 3 1/2 as an important number. (See Daniel 12:7 and Revelation 11:11.) This number was increased twentyfold in the Babylonian captivity, which thus lasted 70 years (20 x 3 1/2). Since the Babylonian captivity was 20 times longer than the punishment in Elijah's time, just so the captivity that comes with falling away from Christ is 20 times longer than the Babylonian captivity, as this sin is more serious than that of fleshly Israel. Hence the 70 years of the Babylonian captivity is multiplied by 20 which yields 1400. Rothmann believed that the fall of the church began after the true church of the apostles had lasted about 100 years following Christ's ascension. Since Jesus was 33 or 34 at the time of His ascension, this sum of time brings one to Rothmann's own day, 1533-34. He was sure that the restitution growing out of the Reformation was the final one. With it the time of suffering and corruption and error were past. The moment of glory and vengeance had dawned. God would now repay the wanton servants of Antichrist — "the seal is broken and the trumpet already blown . . . therefore the God-fearing, the suppressed, the suffering, freely lift up their heads, for their deliverance is not far off!" [2]

The history of Christianity is strewn with the wreckage of just such constructions and clever manipulations of biblical data. The proper response must *not* be that of the scoffers of which Peter writes in his second epistle (3:4) who conclude that, since all things have continued as they were from the creation, therefore there can be no final coming! No, Jesus will in fact return in due time, visibly and in glorious power, but He has not seen fit to give us more than intimations of how it will come to pass. Indeed, our Lord said that even He does not know the time of His return! (See Matthew 24:36 and Mark 13:32.)

The Apostle John gives us reason to believe that Jesus did not intend even those intimations to provide His followers with pieces of a puzzle to put together in an attempt to deduce further information. In fact, on several occasions recorded by John, Jesus indicates that His enigmatic prophecies would be appreciated fully only *after* the event had occurred! In John

14:28, 29 Christ reminded His disciples that He would go away and then come to them again, adding, "And now I have told you before it takes place, so that when it does take place, you may believe." In chapter 16 He concludes His message of exhortation, instruction, and promise (found in chapters 13, 14, and 15) with the recognition that the time is not far off when they will be expelled from the synagogues and even put to death. Jesus says He has told His disciples this in order "that when their [*i.e.*, those who persecuted Me and shall do the same to you] hour comes you may remember that I told you of them" (16:4). The forewarning of such circumstances provides both comfort and endurance for the time when the unwelcome prospect comes to pass.

These two illustrations alert us to something more than a characteristic of Jesus' predictions. They require us not to be simplistic, as though all Scriptures may be readily understood in terms of a simple first or second coming. Rather, as many as five different comings have been identified in Jesus' teachings and messages so that "the coming again of Jesus may thus be conceived as a series of manifestations of His living presence and activity in the world, culminating in a glorious triumph at the Last Day. . . ."³

These five different comings may be described as follows:

(1) His coming after death in bodily resurrection.

(2) His coming in abiding presence initially at

85

Pentecost as the Holy Spirit.

(3) His coming in physical death to take His own to Himself "that where I am there you may be also," or as Paul put it, "to die is gain . . . to depart and be with Christ . . . is far better" (Phil. 1:21, 23).

(4) His coming at great crises of history, such as the destruction of Jerusalem.

(5) The Parousia.

While we are focusing primarily in this study on the last coming, we must always see it in relation to the others. In fact, the middle three comings listed above are continuously in operation in terms of mankind and human history, while the first one will be tied to the fifth when the resurrected Lord returns in glory at the end of history.

The final and most decisive coming is spoken of in terms that unmistakably refer to Jesus' appearance in august splendor and irresistible authority, He will come in the glory of His Father with His angels and reward every man according to his works. Seated on the throne of His glory, He will gather before Him the people of all nations and separate them one from another as a shepherd divides his sheep from his goats. This is the last day marking the termination of the existing order of things when all pretenses will be exposed, obstinate unbelief and ungodliness punished, and faithfulness crowned with its eternal reward.

Christ spoke of His final coming in language of exceptional emphasis and impressiveness. His appearance in celestial majesty at the end of the world will be to perfect the work interrupted by His death but to be renewed and carried on through the ages by His spiritual energy. This will be the supreme manifestation of His glory. It will signal the final triumph of His cause, the complete establishment and consummation of the kingdom of God.

Jesus spoke of the time of His return in relation to the kingdom He came to establish as subject to the law of growth. Jesus saw a preparatory process through which the world would go before He ushers in the kingdom in its full glory. He apparently recognized the natural course of human development as an essential factor in determining the time when the world would be ripe for the final manifestation of His presence and power.

Indeed, it may well be that Jesus was attempting to convey to His disciples the fact that there is not even in God's sovereignty a time set for Christ's return, but that rather God has in His sovereignty actually assigned that momentous event to that day when all of the preparatory conditions have been met. The realization of this condition is left undefined and will be according to His unfathomable wisdom which is revealed to us only in ambiguous glimpses such as the statement, "This gospel of the kingdom will be preached throughout the whole world . . . and then the end will come" (Mt. 24:14). It is doubtful that the nearness of this time of the end can be assessed by analyzing the number of tribes whose languages has not yet been reduced to writing and a portion of

Scripture published in them (even though the work of the Bible societies may be a factor in the process Christ envisioned).

It is equally doubtful that this time can be determined even approximately, as some Christians believe, by preparing a checklist of events which they believe Scriptures indicate will transpire before Christ returns. In fact, there is serious reason to believe that engagement in such an endeavor may bring upon us the rebuke of our Lord. The harsh judgments of those who adhere to such a prophetic system toward those who do not espouse their understanding and timetable may be somewhat comparable to the wickedness which the Lord severely condemned in the servant who, instead of tending to his business, was found mishandling the other servants! (See Luke 12:41-48.)

Christ obviously envisioned some kind of evolution of human affairs in contemplating the triumph of His kingdom even though His faith in that ultimate victory was so real and assured that it seemed to Him imminent. We now must come to terms with the fact that nearly 2,000 years have already passed without His return. Peter provides the key when he reminds us that God's time is not like our time. "With the Lord one day is as a thousand years, and a thousand years as one day" (2 Pet. 3:8). Elton Trueblood has suggested that God's timetable may be so unlike ours that we who are living today may be nearer to the time of the first Christians than to those still living at the time of Christ's return. [4]

Regarding the manner of Christ's return, a considerable number of passages represent it as altogether startling and unexpected. It appears that many Christians today are quite sure that they need not be surprised since they have constructed from the scattered raw materials in God's Word a timetable against which they can check the progress of world affairs and, as it were, know the hour. Yet the fact remains that Jesus explicitly warned that even the most striking and palpable signs might be misread! (See Matthew 24:23-26.) Even the heralds of the great climax must not be taken as the climax itself. "All these things must come to pass, but the end is not yet" (Mt. 24:6, KJV).

Whatever the catastrophic social or other upheavals preceding it, the event is to come suddenly and unexpectedly, at "an hour you do not expect" (Mt. 24:44; see also Lk. 12:40-46). Paul in 1 Thessalonians 5:4 does say, "You are not in darkness, brethren, for that day to surprise you like a thief." But the point seems to be our continual readiness and our faithfulness to the tasks our Lord has given us at all times rather than that we have inside information about the time of His coming. The Lord was concerned that His followers not be duped by false signs. Consequently, He attempted to reassure us that when He does come it shall be dazzlingly, unmistakably evident, thus suggesting that we may ignore those signs with which many are preoccupied since we need not fear that we will miss it!

The decisive significance of the Parousia will be that —

(1) Christ's divine dignity and power shall be fully revealed (Mt. 24:30; 25:31; 26:64; *et al*).

(2) His authority as Judge shall be manifested (Jn. 5:22, 23).

(3) The future destinies of men shall be declared (Mt. 13:41-43; 25:34-46; etc.).

(4) The kingdom shall be cleansed of all things that offend and exalted to its perfection (Mt. 13:41; 24:31).

(5) The existing world order shall come to an end.

Entirely contrary to the elaborate understanding and hopes of many Christians, G. M'Hardy dares to say: "In the teaching of Jesus Himself there is no trace of the thought that the Parousia would inaugurate an outward visible sovereignty on earth, when He would assume the reins of government, and rule as King in the realm of temporal affairs. That thought arose among His followers only at a subsequent period. The idea implied in His utterances is rather that His final glorious advent shall mark the definite close of the long drama of human life on the earth, by the removal of all His true disciples to the heavenly state, and the consignment of the unfaithful to the doom prepared for them. That shall be the last day, when the human race shall have had its full trial under the dispensations of the divine truth and grace — the winding up of the world's history."[5]

One thing yet in closing — a fact so inconspicuously stated in the Scripture that it is doubtful if most Christians have really noticed it. It is a fact that takes us beyond the prospects of the hereafter, whether far or near! Since the topics of this study already stretch our ability to comprehend even dimly those prospects of that world beyond this, it is small wonder that we have seldom given thought to anything that reaches ever farther out into the eternity ahead. But the Spirit saw fit through the writing of the Apostle Paul to tell us one thing about that time beyond even the Parousia and heaven and hell. He reveals that "when all things are subjected to him, then the Son himself will also be subjected to him who put all things under him, that God may be everything to every one" (1 Cor. 15:28).

"Come, Lord Jesus!"

7
FINAL JUDGMENT

Just as the Bible nowhere provides proofs for the existence of God but rather declares and assumes that fact, so nowhere does the Scripture state why it is necessary to take the judgment of God into account. The Scripture instead declares that the judgment will take place and proceeds to speak from a wide variety of perspectives about it. The moral need for a final squaring of accounts, a balancing of the books both positively and negatively, is obvious. If our moral sense is even a pale reflection of God's absolute righteousness (and we believe that it is!), then the many injustices that somehow "get by" man's ability to punish or correct, not to mention the many good deeds that are neither recognized nor rewarded, cry out for fair treatment sometime, somehow.

The idea of God as the final impartial Judge is essential to human thought and experience. The epigram, "To know everything is to pardon everything," is in effect an expression of human helplessness. The cry of David, "Let me fall into the hand of the Lord . . . but let me not fall into the hand of man" (1 Chron. 21:13) is really a cry of humanity forever conscious of the limitations of its own judgments. Experience deepens the sense of ignorance and fallibility attached to our judgments. [1]

The idea of judgment is implicit in government. If a ruler is to have authority and maintain order, he must call transgressors to account. So deeply is this exercise of some kind of sovereignty imbedded in any conception of deity, that the idea of judgment appears to be coextensive with religion. [2]

Although this chapter has to do with final judgment, we must go no further without summarizing the various dimensions of the concept conveyed by the verb and noun "to judge" and "judgment." The common assertion, itself a judgment, made by many Christians, "Now you mustn't judge," cries for clarification in light of the ultimate implications of our topic. Arnold C. Schultz has summarized it well:

The Christian conscience makes ethical judgments unavoidable and imperative. "He that is spiritual judgeth all things" (1 Cor. 2:15). The New Testament seems to teach that a Christian should not judge his brother. Jesus gave the command, "Judge not" (Mt. 7:1). Paul says that he that is spiritual is judged of no man (1 Cor. 2:15). But an examination of the contexts of these passages shows that what Jesus had in mind was that one must not judge another *without first judging oneself*, and that Paul means that a spiritual person cannot be judged by a natural man in spiritual things. It is impossible to make an ethical judgment without passing judgment upon the one who performs the act. [3]

Even though the evil may have been prompted by the subtle workings of the devil and his hosts, the person perpetrating the act must be held responsible for carrying out the evil, just as both the serpent and Adam and Eve were punished for the disobedience in partaking of the forbidden fruit.

The Christian church is admonished to limit its judgment to those who are within. Those who are without are to be left to the judgment of God. (See 1 Corinthians 5:13.) The apostolic writers press upon their readers the duty of discrimination according to certain standards of right and wrong, and not according to human prejudice. The writers assume that those born of the Spirit and living "in Christ" are capable of testing all things and holding to that which is right. They are able to test the spirits to see whether they be of God. (See 1 Thessalonians 5:21 and 1 John 4:1.) The followers of Christ are to pronounce "anathema" on the proclaimer of "another" gospel. They are to refuse hospitality to a false teacher on the ground that a provision for his lodging and food involves a participation in his evil works. (See Galatians 1:8, 9, and 2 John 10. 11.) Whatever is subversive to the person and work of Jesus is to be rejected. Though human judgment is imperfect and limited in capacity, yet such teachings as these delegate to re-generated persons considerable responsibility and privilege. [4]

The line of the Apostles' Creed which says "from thence He shall come to judge the quick and the dead" unmistakably speaks of that great and final judgment which shall be ushered in as a result of the Lord's return. In a sense the intermediate state or near hereafter is already a judgment. However, it is a provisional or temporary one since the final disposition is to be made at some distant and future time. The Parousia presents a scene of surpassing grandeur, extent, and interest. The accompanying judgment stands in the New Testament as the logical terminus of the life of the race which began with Creation. The era of human life on earth demands a judgment as its proper culmination.

One scholar has noted that God established Himself as King at the Creation, and confirmed His kingship in every subsequent mighty act of salvation for His people. (See Exodus 15:18; Psalms 93, 94, 95, and 99; and Isaiah 52:7.) Furthermore, He will set up His kingdom in its fullness at that great day when the consummation of history is accomplished, and the final judgments are pronounced and sealed. (See Isaiah 24 to 26 and Matthew 25:31-46.) We may say that we have a triple "time-content" both for the kingdom of God and for the judgment of God in these respects:

1. He established Himself as both King and Judge at the beginning.

2. He continues to manifest His kingship and judgship at every crisis in history.

3. He will become King and Judge at the great crisis which marks the end of history. (Indeed, "crisis" is the Greek word for "judgment.")[5]

The judgment is often believed to be cosmic in character, involving the extraterrestrial vastness of the universe and not simply the earth alone. The focus of Scripture, however, is predominantly upon the earth. Unlike modern Western thought, the Bible does not dissociate the moral plane from the physical and natural plane. The condemnation of man by God is affecting not only man's conscience, but his entire existence, internally and externally. His mind is darkened (Rom. 1:21, 22), his body succumbs to sickness and death (Rom. 6:23; 1 Cor. 11:30), and his natural setting is in bondage to decay (Rom. 8:19-23). How far the curse of sin reached beyond this planet is not as clear as the profound extent to which it has affected the natural and spiritual realities of human life as we know it.

Judgment in the New Testament has a double meaning (except for several passages in the writings of John where "to judge" means simply "to condemn"). Judgment is expressed positively in terms such as joy in the presence of the Master, the blessing of the Father, entrance into the kingdom of God, life eternal, glory, honor, immortality, peace, and rest. Negatively, the term is also used to refer to such consequences as outer darkness, where there will be weeping and gnashing of teeth, where the worm does not die and the fire is not quenched, everlasting fire, separation from God, wrath and indignation, distress and anguish, eternal perdition, and affliction. It is not at all uncommon for the Old Testament to speak of Israel's salvation as a judgment, when the meaning is one of joy in victory and reward, just as it may also speak of the corollary punishment of those outside the covenant who are Israel's (and God's) enemies. For God's people the judgment of the world by the Flood was an event of salvation and deliverance, as was also the judgment upon Sodom and on Egypt. The judgment of God on behalf of His people is thought of as an acquittal, since judgment on the one hand is deliverance and victory. (See Isaiah 30:18.) On the other hand, it is a punishment for those not His people. (See 2 Corinthians 2:16.) [6]

In the Old Testament, God delegates His functions of Judge on earth in part to the coming messianic Prince who is destined to establish His kingdom. As the idea of "the day of the Lord" developed, this concept tended to merge with that of the coming Messiah, also called Son of Man, and He was to be the Judge of all men. By the time of the New Testament and the early creeds of the church, it is roundly declared that Christ will "come again with glory to judge both the quick and the dead" (Nicene Creed, circa AD 381.) This association of ideas was the expectation of the New Testament writers generally, with the exception of

John. The Synoptic Gospels set forth a multitude of tests which furnish ground for continuous judgment in this life, as well as in the last judgment. The Gospel of John is more concerned with the inner and hidden judgment which is being pronounced continually in man's soul. John's view does not conflict with the concept of the last judgment but rather emphasizes another dimension.

The fact that judgment is being meted out, whether continuously or in a final judgment, is a revelation of God's mercy. It might be imagined that God would create the world, set it in motion along the lines of certain "laws," and that he would not intervene. One might expect Him to allow the world to corrupt itself increasingly until it brought about its own destruction. But the New Testament declares that a judgment is on its way which cannot be escaped by anyone, past or present. This is so because God in His mercy has not been ready to abandon men to their own destruction. Rather, He "so loved the world that he gave his only Son, that whoever believes in him should not perish but have eternal life" (Jn. 3:16). The salvation of those who believe and accept God's offer has value and meaning only if all who refuse to be reconciled with God are denied entrance into His kingdom. The ultimate objective of God's love is not simply the continued intermixing of the wicked with those committed to righteousness, in which case no final judgment would be necessary. No, God will see things through to an ultimate victory. While

God is long-suffering in order that all men may come to repentance (Lk. 13:6-9; Rom. 2:4; 2 Pet. 3:9), yet He is not infinitely long-suffering. In due time He will come and separate the righteous from the unrighteous. God is committed, however, to having His gospel declared throughout the earth before He returns to execute His judgment. (See Matthew 24:14.) In fact, we are told that all the saints from time immemorial are being held in waiting until God chooses to climax the life of this world with the rendering of His rewards and punishments. (See Hebrews 11:40.)

The last judgment will be in accordance with "the law" and man's attachment to Jesus. Jesus says that He did not come to abolish the law but rather to deepen our understanding of it and to emphasize what is essential. (See Matthew 5:17-48; 22:37-40; and Romans 13:8-10.) Jesus presents Himself as the supreme and personal test. What a man's attitude is toward the law is revealed by his attitude toward God, the Lawgiver, as He is revealed to us in His Son. Our attitude is obvious from our deeds and words. This kind of judgment is continuous and cumulative in this life but comes to final fruition at the last judgment. Jesus has left us a substantial number of varied and concrete tests for training us in true godliness. (See footnote 7 for a listing of many of these tests.) They cover almost every phase of human life, both inward and outward. Judgments are continuous in the sphere of our moral lives, as our consciences persistently affirm. No one can plead ignorance of many of these. Each of us shall be judged impartially and righteously. Jesus offers Himself as the supreme standard of life. The work of the invisible Holy Spirit which Jesus sent to replace His physical presence among men convicts men of sin, of righteousness, and of judgment. (See John 16:7-9.) He accomplishes this by showing men their unlikeness to Christ. The gospel concerning Jesus is to be preached in all the world so that His character may continually challenge people and serve as the measure of the judgment they pass upon themselves by their response.

In all the Gospels, judgment is determined by the relation which a man holds to Jesus Christ and this continuous judgment will culminate in a final judgment. The inadequacy and inequalities of punishment in this life demand a final adjustment for all persons to achieve ultimate justice. The story of the rich man and Lazarus suggests the lines along which this final accounting will be made and how the equitable readjustments are accomplished even though the story is not in itself a picture of the last judgment. It is clear that the proper rewards and penalties do not fully result from the continuous judgment in this life, and that the final balances will need to be struck after death. (See 1 Timothy 5:24.)

Obviously our professed attachment to Christ's person and kingdom will not be acceptable unless it is genuine in His sight. (See Matthew 7:21-23 and Luke 13:25-27.) This may prove to be quite in contrast to our own judgment. Its substance must be something more than words. (See 1 John 3:18.) The living example of Jesus during His earthly life, the guidance of the Scripture, and the empowering of the Holy Spirit are more helpful in ascertaining the authenticity of our Christian experience than the law. Paul teaches that the norm of the law is superseded by that of the Spirit of Christ. (See Romans 8:1-17; Galatians 5:13-25; and 6:7-9.) This does not eliminate the necessity of works since, whether in the sight of the law or of Christ, God intends that we live our faith, not simply mouth orthodox words. Consequently, the Apostle Paul speaks of "the day of wrath when God's righteous judgment will be revealed. For he will render to every man according to his works" (Rom. 2:5, 6; *cf.* 2 Cor. 5:10). The works by which we shall each be judged will not be considered in isolation, but rather according to the testimony they give to the depths and direction of our character.

Final judgment belongs naturally to God but God entrusts its administration to Christ at His appearance in glory. (See Matthew 3:11, 12; 13:41-43; and John 5:22.) The "day of judgment" (Mt. 10:15; 12:36; 2 Pet. 2:9; 1 Jn. 4:17) and the "day of the Lord" (1 Cor. 1:8; 1 Thess. 5:2; Heb. 10:25) are one and the same. There is no sufficiently convincing reason to follow the Darby-Scofield line of thought which distinguishes different judgments taking place at different times, for different purposes, and involving different people.[8] Such a view seems

101

more novel than perceptive, more complicated than clear, and more distracting than helpful.

The subjects of the final judgment will be all mankind, past and present. The reference to "all the nations" (Mt. 25:32) is understood to be equivalent to the mention of all men. (See John 5:27-29; Matthew 12:36; Romans 14:10; and Revelation 12:12, 13.) It can be inferred from Matthew 8:29 that evil spirits will also be judged. However, it seems proper to understand this as a reference to their consignment to the place prepared for the devil and his angels, since their judgment may be assumed to have taken place when they chose to join the rebellion against God in some primeval day. If this interpretation is correct, it is the counterpart to the holy angels not coming into judgment, since they have continued throughout the age to accompany and serve the Holy Judge. (See Matthew 16:27 and 25:31.) Only where there is both the need for redemption and the possibility of it is a final judgment called for.

There remains yet two major aspects of our topic to speak to : (1) What of the heathen who have never had any opportunity to hear of Christ and His salvation? (2) Are there different degrees of punishment to which God will consign the wicked?

Whether more out of curiosity or compassion, the nature of the judgment and destiny of the wicked is an old and popular topic. If the gospel of Christ is for the whole world, as we believe it is, we cannot help wondering about those who were destroyed by God's decree in Old Testament times (Deut. 7:1, 2, for example). And what about those in some obscure part of the world who for generations, if not millennia, lay beyond the reach of knowledge of those who knew of God's plan for man's salvation. Since they scarcely could have rejected a Christ of whom they had not heard, what will be the basis of their judgment? Keep in mind that God's judgment will be both righteous and impartial. The very nature of God is such that Abraham could say, "Shall not the Judge of all the earth do right?" (Gen. 18:25). But we are sobered to recall that as far as Sodom and Gomorrah were concerned, God's doing right meant that they were both utterly destroyed! Abraham's plea was for the righteous and God responded to his cry. But for the unrepentant wicked, it is frightening to contemplate what is right in God's sight!

We have already learned that God judges on the basis of His revealed will. Since this has not been uniform for all, God's judgment will need to be tempered accordingly. This is precisely what the Scriptures tell us. Romans 2:12 says, "All who have sinned without the law will also perish without the law, and all who have sinned under the law will be judged by the law." It can be assumed that no one will be condemned for rejecting a Christ whom they had no opportunity to accept, or for failing to respond to light they did not have. Rather, such persons will be condemned for not living up to whatever light they did have. Paul also comments, "We know that the judgment of God rightly falls upon those [the heathen] who do such things" (Rom. 2:2). Peter's observation, "Truly I perceive that God shows no partiality, but in every nation any one who fears him and does what is right is acceptable to him" (Acts 10:34, 35), assures us that all will be judged by the deepest principles and not by any superficialities. We have already noted that God will render to every man according to his deeds, whether good or bad, and also that He will do so "according to what a man has, not according to what he has not" (2 Cor. 8:12).

This is but another way of stating what Paul says in another place. When God reveals the hidden motives of the heart, "then every man will receive his commendation from God" (1 Cor. 4:5).[9] When we recall once more that God is not willing that any should perish, the somewhat involved statement of C. W. Hale Amos is comforting:

> If God will have all men to be saved, we are surely led to infer that no man in the world, whether heathen or half-heathen in point of knowledge and privileges, shall be condemned eternally, in whose character there is not found something morally equivalent to that wilful rejection of a free and finished salvation, which alone can seal the doom of those who hear with full intelligence the gospel's joyful sound. From what we know respecting the terms of our own salvation, we are led irresistibly to the conclusion that no man can perish except by his own fault and deliberate choice.[10]

As to whether there will be differing degrees of punishment in God's judgment, various scriptural passages suggest an answer. Luke 12:47, 48 tells us: "That servant who knew his master's will, but did not make ready or act according to his will, shall receive a severe beating. But he who did not know, and did what deserved a beating, shall receive a light beating. Every one to whom much is given, of him will much be required; and of him to whom men commit much they will demand the more."[11] The latter sentence is of particular interest. Other passages, such as the following, also deserve consideration:

Woe to you, Chorazin! woe to you, Bethsaida! for if the mighty works done in you had been done in Tyre and Sidon, they would have repented long ago in sackcloth and ashes. But I tell you, it shall be more tolerable on the day of judgment for Tyre and Sidon than for you. Matthew 11:21, 22.

The queen of the South will arise at the judgment with the men of this generation and condemn them; for she came from the ends of the earth to hear the wisdom of Solomon, and behold, something greater than Solomon is here. The men of Nineveh will arise at the judgment with this generation and condemn it; for they repented at the preaching of Jonah, and behold, something greater than Jonah is here. Luke 11:31, 32.

A man who has violated the law of Moses dies without mercy at the testimony of two or three witnesses. How much worse punishment do you think will be deserved by the man who has spurned the Son of God? Hebrews 10:28, 29.

In these passages our human inclination and sense of fairness, however faulty, is affirmed as fundamentally sound. It is interesting to note that our Lord compared the response of two cities contemporary with Him with two ancient cities that were destroyed by Alexander and Artaxerxes III respectively in the mid-300s BC. Jesus dared to manifest the omniscience of the Judge God intends Him to be in the future when He stated what the response of these two ancient cities would have been had they enjoyed the privileges that Chorazin and Bethsaida did in fact have. Some scholars suggest that God, in His treatment of the heathen, will reward or punish them in light of what their response would have been had they heard the gospel! If such is the case, then surely our God is indeed a gracious God to take such considerations into account in His effort to spare everyone any unfair penalty.

In conclusion regarding this question, consider the words of S. D. F. Salmond:

> The principle of degrees in reward and punishment must to taken in all its breadth as an essential and qualifying element in the doctrine in question. The idea of reward proportioned to the measure of service, and penalty proportioned to the measure of failure occupies a much larger place in Christ's teachings and in

106

the New Testament generally than is usually recognized. The issue to each will be in equitable accordance with the possession of talent, opportunity, and knowledge. The doctrine of degrees is the relief given us by Christ Himself in thinking of the maladjustments of the present existence, the mystery of unequal circumstances, and the lot of the lost. It provides for all possible graduations in the punitive awards of the future.[12]

Just as there is no other entrance into the near hereafter except through the gate of death, so there is no entrance into the far hereafter except through what Emil Brunner called "the narrow pass of judgment."

8

THE DARK SIDE OF THE FAR HEREAFTER

If you think I'm indulging in a euphemism in the title of this chapter because the traditional doctrine of hell is a painful and unpleasant subject, you are partly right. But my choice of title arises more out of substance than from squeamishness. It might have been phrased "The Dark Side of Eternity," but since the duration of the biblical words are somewhat in question, it seems better to avoid such an absolute connotation as "eternity" suggests in favor of a more ambiguous, but accurate concept. I am indebted to J. Paterson-Smyth's chapter on hell in his book *The Gospel of the Hereafter* referred to earlier. To neither add nor subtract from what the Scriptures teach is our goal. We cannot afford to settle for less than "the way, the truth, and the life," which our Lord has offered to us in Himself.

Beyond the final judgment is either reward or punishment. In that great day, all who have ever lived who bear the image of God in their beings will stand before their Creator

to give an account of their stewardship. (See
Matthew 12:36; Luke 16:2; and Romans 14:12.)
Beyond the hints the Bible gives us of this
far hereafter lies only mystery and the confidence that the Judge of all the earth shall do
right. Compared to our questions, the biblical revelation is not only sparing in quantity,
but limited and somewhat ambiguous in vocabulary, and our understanding is at best
finite and frequently dull.

Some older Christians complain that scarcely
anyone preaches hellfire and brimstone as
they used to do! The implication is that preachers today are not made of the same stuff that
ministers used to be. Cowardice or liberalism
are sometimes cited to account for this. It can
be one of these, of course, but there may be
better reasons. Perhaps there is a troublesome
defect in the traditional view or perhaps the
hellishness of contemporary warfare has dulled
the shock effect which that kind of preaching
would have today. We are admonished to "speak
the truth in love" and one may question how
the preachers of old could describe the terrors
of hell with such relish. In any case, we intend
to make a full investigation of what the Scriptures say on this subject, especially in the New
Testament. It may turn out that we shall need
to be less opinionated and judgmental once we
have become sufficiently informed of what the
Scripture does not say.

It is quite important that scriptural truths
be expressed in a language that conveys what
the Bible tells us as faithfully as possible. It

is unfortunate if we persist in using the terminology of an old and beloved version such as the King James long after those same English words no longer mean what they did in 1611 when that version was first published.[1]

We noticed in an earlier chapter that those who pass through death into the intermediate state enter into a condition that approximates to some extent their ultimate destination, whether of happiness or torment. We now wish to look especially at the prospects of those who die outside of Christ. One of the key words we shall be dealing with is "Gehenna" (not "Hades," which is simply a cover-all word for the place of the dead in general). The topic of our particular interest here is that place of conscious and terrible torment in which all the unrighteous will find themselves following the judgment. Of all the topics we have discussed so far, this is the most dreadful.

Many Scriptures leave us with the strong impression that there is only irrevocable ruin and loss in store for those not eligible for reward. In spite of God's love and patience extended toward all men while on earth, these people seem at last to have thumbed their noses at all the promptings given them by the Holy Spirit to repentance and faith, prostituted everything good, thrown the weight of their lives to the side of sin and selfishness, and so have passed the point of no return. The judgment scene which Christ described has clearly a ring of terrible horror, if not finality, about it.

At this point the simplest and safest thing to do would be to rehearse the traditional view of evangelical Christianity. Many Christians, perhaps most of us, are simply content to follow the party line. If this leaves some biblical data unaccounted for, we protect ourselves either by saying that not all of us can be theologians or we take comfort in the fact that "this is the way we have been taught!" The cults have a way of sleuthing out what they hold to be inconsistencies in the historic Christian doctrines and needling us with questions and counterviews. We may respond by drawing our doctrinal coat about us even tighter, hoping they will go away, or we may examine the Scripture again and discover that we have drawn conclusions that resolve what the Scripture leaves ambiguous. Frequently the cults are guilty of this latter practice also, but this does not excuse us in doing so. Apparently many people cannot be satisfied with a faith which leaves some questions open or only partially answered. The longer I am a Christian, and the more I study the Scriptures, the firmer my faith becomes in the major Christian doctrines. I can say this even though there emerge a few issues and questions on which I am less sure than when I first believed as a teenager. At the same time I am becoming more sure than ever that the God I serve and love and worship is so great and so good and so loving that He may be trusted to do all things right whether or not it is according to my very human and fallible judgment!

Our goal in all Bible study is to take all the biblical material into account as responsibly as possible before we decide what the Scripture teaches on a given topic. No view should be accepted as entirely trustworthy or satisfactory which leaves any of the data unaccounted for. Granted, the best we often are able to do is to adopt the view which is more satisfactory than another even if it does not account for everything neatly. We should expect to "grow in the grace and knowledge of Our Lord" as Peter admonishes (2 Pet. 3:18). Our minds must always remain open to more light since the same Spirit who inspired the Scriptures is still alive and at work among Christians. We must always remain open to the possibility that He can and will lead us to some new and unexpected insights without adding to or subtracting from the Scriptures.

Essentially the same three views are abroad today on this topic that have been around for centuries. The first and least satisfactory one we might call *modified annihilationism*. This holds that only the righteous shall live on and that all evil doers and unbelievers shall ultimately be destroyed. Some verses in the Bible strongly suggest this view but few, if any, of these are found in the New Testament. Most Christians reject this approach entirely. Maimonides, a great Jewish scholar of the Middle Ages, expressed this view well for all who hold it: "The punishment of the wicked is that they will not merit . . . life [in the world to come] but will be utterly cut off in their death. Whoever

112

does not merit . . . life is a dead thing who will never live but is cut off in his wickedness and perishes like an animal."[2]

A second view is frequently referred to as *universalism.* There are several varieties of this view. Christians too often fail to distinguish between these varieties and simply reject the popular caricature of universalism indiscriminately. There is a variety of universalism for which little more can be said than that it results from a namby-pamby view of sin and a sentimentalized view of God's goodness, but there is also a variety of universalism that takes the Scriptures and sin seriously. Admittedly, this latter view does not take some terms in the absolute sense that evangelicalism does, but it does not explain away or minimize the reality of sin and Satan or the awfulness of the punishment that is the consequence of disobedience and unbelief.

This is not the time or place to examine more fully the strengths and weaknesses of this view, though there are implications concerning it which will be touched upon in the material to follow. It has roots in some of the same deep questions which Judaism and Christianity have both felt. The Jewish author C. G. Montefiore has expressed one of these tersely indeed: "How anyone can believe in eternal punishment . . . or in any soul which God has made being 'lost,' and also believe in the love, nay, even in the justice, of God is a mystery indeed."[3] Paul, the converted Jewish rabbi, wrote, "Love never ends" (1 Cor. 13:8). One is faced with the mind-boggling situation of understanding what love can mean if a person made in God's image may be consigned with absolute finality to endless torment! Paul's words in Philippians 2:9-11 speak of a time when "at the name of Jesus every knee should bow, in heaven and on earth and under the earth, and every tongue confess that Jesus Christ is Lord, *to the glory of God the Father*" (emphasis mine). This presents a situation which for some Christians defies sensible meaning since they cannot conceive of a confession of Christ being to God's glory unless it is freely and joyfully made! [4]

The third view, which most Christians hold, we shall call *everlasting punishment*. It does stand upon a sturdy base. Alan Richardson says succinctly, "It is impossible to soften the severity of Jesus' warning against unrepented sin, and the sentimentalism which seeks to do so is a distortion of the teaching of Jesus and the New Testament as a whole. Whatever may be implied by the symbolism of 'unquenchable fire' (Mk. 9:43) or 'eternal fire' (Mt. 18:8, *cf.* 25:41) or the casting of the wicked into the 'furnace of fire' (Mt. 3:42, 50), we have no right to explain the symbolism away." [5] The wicked, according to the New Testament, are those who have heard the gospel and ignored or rejected it as well as those who have not responded even to the natural revelation they have had. The Scriptures clearly teach that a mysterious and awful malignity attaches to sin and that persisting in sin brings one to utter ruin. No arguments about the love and power of God can soften the fact that man's free will is exercised at a terrible risk if it is in rebellion against God.

Yet, on the other hand, running through all this background of darker hue in Scripture is a curious golden thread — a thread that suggests that evil shall not be eternal in God's universe. Many thoughtful minds shrink from the idea that evil shall be as permanent as good in the ultimate plan of a holy God. Many cringe at the thought that any evil power should exist unendingly side-by-side with Him who is utterly righteous, even though that existence be "in chains." There seems inevitably in such a case to be the implication of unending resistance to God and hatred of righteousness even if the hatred and resistance are both under God's sovereignty. But then if wickedness is shackled and helpless, perhaps even its presence is a testimony to God's majesty and power. At this point our ability to reason, our sense of logic, begins to quiver and quake.

The big question is whether such a situation would fulfill those hints in the Scripture of a time when God shall be all-in-all and everything shall be restored to its God-intended beauty and function. (See 1 Corinthians 15:28; Ephesians 1:23; and Acts 3:21.) Charles T. P. Grierson struggles with this nagging question: "As regards the predicted bliss of the pardoned, there can be no doubt that Jesus taught that it was of eternal duration, for that bliss is naught but the gift of life, and that life is the life of God Himself, and so necessarily is ever-lasting as He is everlasting. (See John 1:4 and 5:26-29; *cf.* 1 John 5:11, 12.) His teaching regarding the duration of the punishment of the wicked, however, is less plain. Much of His language is highly figurative, and may have been used by Him only to express the terrible punishment that awaits unrepented sin in the next world, without precluding the hope that God will finally win all to Himself by love; a hope that not a few passages in the later books of the New Testament suggest."[6]

Let us lay this dilemma aside for a while as we bring into focus some additional data. We must look carefully at the use and meaning of the words translated "damn" and "damnation" and "eternal" and "everlasting."

The words "damn" and "damnation" convey to us the idea of doom to a hell of unending torment. The original word conveyed no such meaning either to our Lord or to the apostles. Neither did it convey such a concept to the translators of the Authorized Version. When they translated the Greek word *krino* and *katakrino* by the English words "damn" and "damnation," they did not at all mean what we understand them to mean. The word *krino* simply means "to judge," and *katakrino* means "to judge adversely" or "to condemn." Surely the translators did not think so evil of God as to believe that He could never judge a man without condemning him, and that if He did in some cases judge a man adversely, that it was always to everlasting torment. Not at all.

116

As a matter of fact, the whole concept of judgment has quite a different base and extent than that.[7]

In 2 Corinthians 5:10 it says, "For we must all appear before the judgment seat of Christ, so that each one may receive good or evil, according to what he had done in the body." Judgment then can as readily be the basis for our reward as it can be the basis for our torment. In John 5:28, 29 our Lord pointed out that the Father has granted authority to the Son to execute judgment because He is the Son of Man. "Do not marvel at this," Jesus said, "for the hour is coming when all who are in the tombs will hear His voice and come forth, those who have done good, to the resurrection of life, and those who have done evil, to the resurrection of judgment." They will be called out of their graves to be judged and rewarded whether for good or evil.

The English word "damn" at the time of the translation of the King James Version in 1611 had no such awful and final meaning as it has now. It simply meant "to judge," without the strongly negative connotation it has today. When we say to someone, "Now you are judging," it always has a negative connotation. We are verbally slapping somebody's fingers. Or we say, "We're not supposed to judge," which is itself a judgment. We are stating a negative opinion. Rather, we ought to know that one of the things the presence of the Holy Spirit in our lives gives us is a perceptive ability to judge, *i.e.*, to discern good from evil.

John Wycliffe's translation of the story of the woman taken in adultery illustrates well the point we are making. In the Wycliffe translation, Jesus said, "Woman, hath no man damned thee?" He did not mean at all, "Hath no man condemned thee [katakrino] to eternal punishment." The woman said, "No man, Lord." And then in the Wycliffe translation Jesus says, "Neither do I damn [katakrino] thee." The English word "damn" at that time meant only "to condemn adversely." But it has nothing to do with a place of eternal and everlasting torment.

Words are unstable and tend to change their meaning with the passing of time. And so in the 360 plus years since the King James Version was translated a different, darker, more ominous, and final connotation has overtaken this originally milder English word.

The revisers of the Scripture and the newer translations have largely, if not entirely, omitted the words "damn" or "damnation." But so many of us still read and know the King James best that the error persists.

Did our Lord say, "He that believeth not shall be damned," in the sense in which we tend to use and understand damn? No! He said, "He that believeth not shall be judged," which is something quite different. Christ said any man would be judged adversely for willfully disbelieving. He simply stated the fact that it shall catch up with him. The person who believes not shall be condemned, but "to what" or "for how long" was not part of His statement. I might judge you or you might judge me adversely for doing a selfish or malicious act, but that would hardly mean that I am committing you or you are committing me to endless punishment.

Again, did Jesus say to those who had done evil that they would rise to the resurrection of damnation? No! He said to the resurrection of judgment. They will be brought back and given an imperishable body. Then with everybody who has ever lived, all in their imperishable bodies, they shall be judged. Did St. Paul say in speaking about eating certain meats, "He that doubteth is damned if he eats," *i.e.,* is doomed to eternal torment if he eats? No, he said such a person is judged adversely if he eats. There is no thought at all in these Scriptures of an endless hell. This brings us to the next set of words we must examine.

A similar situation exists with the texts involving the word "hell." Three Greek words are translated "hell." *Hades* is used 11 times in the Scripture, *Gehenna* 12 times, and *Tartarus* only once. Hades is the name of a god of the underworld. This underworld, thought of as the place of the dead, originally did not speak to the point of whether the place or the people in it were good or bad. It was simply the place of the dead as contrasted to the land of the living. When Christ told the story of the rich man in hell, He had to specify that the rich man was "in torment" (Lk. 16:23), to clarify the situation more precisely. The poor man, also in Hades, was in "Abraham's bosom"

(v. 22). Or again, Peter's sermon on Pentecost Day included these lines which are quoted as a prophecy of Christ, "He was not abandoned to Hades, nor did his flesh see corruption" (Acts 2:31). Or in Revelation 1:18 Christ is saying, "I have the keys of Death and Hades," *i.e.*, the fact of death and the place of the dead.

The next word is *Gehenna*. Gehenna is the Valley of Hinnom. Geographically it is a place just outside the wall of Jerusalem, a ravine, which became a garbage dump. The bodies of criminals and any bodies that were not claimed were deposited (buried is too good a word) in this garbage dump. This very specific place outside Jerusalem was the original Gehenna.

Later popular Jewish belief held that the last judgment was to occur at Gehenna. Since it had the appearance of a terrible place with fire burning continually, consuming the rubbish, it was an appropriate word-picture of the worst that people could imagine. They used the word to describe the place where the last judgment was to occur.

In the Gospels Gehenna is a place of punishment in the next life. The word implies no time factor. It is very imprecise as to place or duration. The word does not give us any information about where it is or how long it will last. It is simply the description of a terrible place.

In Matthew 23:15 our Lord told the Pharisees that they traverse land and sea to make a convert, a proselyte, and when he is made one he is twofold more the child of Gehenna than before. In Matthew 10:28 Christ told His followers to fear him who is able to destroy both soul and body in Gehenna. At another place He spoke of "the damnation of hell," that is, the judgment of Gehenna. Mark 9:48 speaks of Gehenna as a place "where their worm does not die, and the fire is not quenched."

The third word translated as hell is *Tartarus*. It is used only once: "For . . . God did not spare the angels when they sinned, but cast them into hell [*Tartarus*] and committed them to pits of nether gloom to be kept until the judgment" (2 Pet. 2:4). The point is that Tartarus is the place where the wicked angels are kept until the judgment. It is not the place of their confinement after having already been judged. They are kept there reserved in everlasting chains as Jude put it, *until* the judgment. Then they will be brought forth as a criminal is summoned from his jail cell to be judged.

Admittedly, something extremely stern and terrible was meant by these words. Our Lord simply utilized Jewish terminology without defining words. How can we know what He meant? How can we know what Shakespeare means by a certain word? The only way we come to such an understanding is by reading all the writings in which it occurs and discovering what the people of the times understood by the way the word was used. This kind of investigation has been made regarding the use of Gehenna in Jewish writings between 300 BC and AD 300. Only two passages in all the places this word is used outside of the Scripture could be taken to indicate that the Jews understood Gehenna as a place of everlasting torment. The vast majority of the usages clearly do not refer to a never-ending place. [8]

Now what does one do with this kind of evidence? Granted, these citations have less than final authority for us because they are from material other than the Scripture. However, since Christ nowhere clearly defined His words, we can only assume He used words familiar to His hearers in the sense in which they would understand them. They would expect a terrible doom. And isn't that enough? Can anyone say that they would have understood Him to mean absolutely endless torment? It is possible that we have pushed a more extreme and dogmatic meaning because we have not been content with the point our Lord intended. We have pushed it a step beyond that which we have any right or basis to do.

We should also examine the group of texts using the words "everlasting," "eternal," or "forever and ever." These are translations of two words, *aidios* and *aionios*. *Aidios* is used twice in the New Testament; *aionios* appears 71 times. The latter is an adjective derived from the noun *aion* which corresponds to our word "aeon" or "eon." It means an age, an epoch, a long period of time, but certainly not endless. It cannot mean eternity, for Paul repeatedly uses it in the plural. If an aeon is endless, why would you say aeons? Paul repeatedly speaks of "the ages." Popular scientific language refers to "the ice age" and "the stone age" and "the iron age." So the Bible speaks of "this age" or "the coming age" or "the end of the age." "The coming age" means that the age we're in is a passing one and at some point another era will begin. Paul says in Ephesians 3:11 that God's purpose is the purpose of *the ages*. He says in Ephesians 1 that Christ's name is above every name not only in this age but also in the age to come, indicating the conclusion of one age and the beginning of another. In Ephesians 2:7 he says, "That in the coming ages He might show the immeasurable riches of his grace in his kindness toward us in Christ Jesus."

From this noun comes the adjective translated "eternal" meaning "agelong" or "belonging to the ages," depending on whether it is singular or plural. It just does not mean endless or everlasting. Sometimes it may be translated that way but only when the meaning is inherent in the noun that is qualified. In the Septuagint, which our Lord and the apostles frequently quoted, this word is applied to things that have already ended.

I came across this first some years ago in reading Genesis 17. I had read the passage often but one day the word "everlasting" hit me with new force. Speaking of the rite of circumcision, verses 10 and 11 read, "This is my covenant, which you shall keep, between me and you and your descendants after you: Every male among you shall be circumcised. You shall be circumcised in the flesh of your foreskins." Then God says in verse 13, "So shall my covenant be in your flesh an ever-lasting covenant." Everlasting covenant? Cir-cumcision as a rite of the covenant has been annulled for nearly 2,000 years! And yet the word "everlasting" is used.

Interestingly enough, this same word appears in Isaiah 9:6, "And his name will be called . . . Everlasting Father." Young, in his trans-lation of the Old Testament, rendered this "Fa-ther of Eternity," which more accurately leaves the meaning of "eternity" ambiguous. What-ever eternity is, Christ is the Father of it. The verse is noncommittal regarding its length. The Scriptures also refer to the priesthood of Aaron as *everlasting*, yet we know that it has long been superseded. The temple at Jerusalem was to stand *everlastingly*. It crumbled into rubble centuries ago. The daily offerings were to be *everlasting*. They have long since been aban-doned. The word clearly means agelong, but it must not be taken to mean something more than it says. One of the most comprehensive of Greek lexicons (Arndt and Gingrich) says of this Greek word that it means "a very long time," "of time gone by" or "of time to come." And then it says, "which, *if it has no end*, is also known as eternity." The lexicon will not say that it ever has the meaning of endlessness. It leaves that in obscurity. As for the Hebrew counterpart the lexicon says "prac-tically eternity." That is to say, for all prac-tical purposes (speaking generally, imprecisely), the word means eternity.

The other word *aidios* is used two times, once

in Romans and again in Jude. It is not used of any human being who has ever lived. One case refers to God and the other to angels. Romans 1:20 reads, "Ever since the creation of the world his invisible nature, namely, his eternal [*aidios*] power, and deity, has been clearly perceived in the things that have been made." And Jude 1:6 says, "And the angels that did not keep their own position but left their proper dwelling have been kept by him in eternal [*aidios*] chains in the nether gloom until the judgment of the great day." Even here there is a qualification. They are kept there *until the judgment*.

A few additional passages must be noted that cannot readily be harmonized with the considerations we have just reviewed. We have noted that our Lord may have been trying to impress us in every way with the urgency of turning *from* sin and *to* His obedience while we have persisted in construing His words as speaking rather to the ultimate destiny of sinful men. This, we have suggested, is similar to the disciples asking when Christ would restore the earthly kingdom to Israel while Christ taught that His kingdom was near but not of this world.

But all this does not clearly account for such verses as Matthew 12:31, 32, "Therefore I tell you, every sin and blasphemy will be forgiven men, but the blasphemy against the Spirit will not be forgiven. And whoever says a word against the Son of man will be forgiven; but whoever speaks against the Holy

Spirit will not be forgiven, either in this age or in the age to come." And Hebrews 6:4, 6, "For it is impossible to restore again to repentance those who have once been enlightened. . . . if they then commit apostasy." Or 10:26, 27. "For if we sin deliberately after receiving the knowledge of the truth, there no longer remains a sacrifice for sins, but a fearful prospect of judgment, and a fury of fire which will consume the adversaries." Or 1 John 5:16 (NEB), "If a man sees his brother committing a sin which is not a deadly sin, he should pray to God for him, and he will grant him life — that is, when men are not guilty of deadly sin. There is such a thing as deadly sin, and I do not suggest that he should pray about that; but although all wrongdoing is sin, not all sin is deadly sin." The presence of this strain of teaching does not necessarily invalidate the other things we have already pointed out, yet these verses most definitely cannot readily be correlated with them.

How can we draw any conclusions regarding our study? We must not force the considerations a little here and there to make them fit our preconceptions.

This should help us understand why responsible Christian scholars feel they must in all honesty caution us regarding the popular evangelical view. J. Burnier says:

> The adjective eternal which is used . . . does not indicate, as in our language, an infinite duration, but denotes that we are dealing with

matters resulting from the final intervention of God, when He will establish the new world. If life in the kingdom is without end and participates in the perpetuity of God, it does *not* follow that the suffering of the reprobate must be prolonged indefinitely. Moreover, every attempt to determine exactly what awaits men beyond judgment comes up against the undefined nature of a concept which was elaborated not to satisfy our curiosity, but to cause us to fear the God who offers us His pardon and eternal life in the fellowship of His Son. Thus the manner in which the New Testament makes use of the notion of judgment concerning heaven and hell; it leads us rather to live this present hour in the faith and obedience to God of Jesus Christ.[8]

Our Lord's concern and that of the New Testament is not that we have a completely clear understanding of what God will do with evil men, but rather that we realize what Jesus tried to help Peter understand when Peter inquired about the future of John. Jesus replied, "What is that to you? Follow me!" (Jn. 21:22). While what we have said about the meanings of certain key words may be true, it does not necessarily explain for us those verses where similar ideas are taught without the use of those words! Perhaps our Lord would say to us regarding our curiosity on this topic that He has many things to tell us but we cannot bear them now! The history of Christianity is not very convincing that Christ's followers have grown beyond many of the same chronic misconceptions that plagued the first Twelve. Perhaps our Lord would reassure us as He did His Twelve when He said, "The hour is coming when I shall no longer speak to you in figures but tell you plainly of the Father" (Jn. 16:25). So long as we persist in asking the wrong questions we shall be divided over the meaning of the answers we think we find in the Scriptures.

Our study has not left us with the certainty in every respect that we may desire or feel we need. What we have found may be unsettling for some. It may tempt them to reject what has been said to avoid the painfulness of a more thorough examination of their personal faith. Hebrews 12:27 speaks of a time when both earth and heaven will be shaken so that the shakable things may be removed and the unshakable things may remain. This may be intolerably threatening for some even while it is deeply reassuring to others. Yet the writer reminds us that in "receiving a kingdom that cannot be shaken . . . , let us offer to God acceptable worship, with reverence and awe; for our God is a consuming fire" (12:28, 29).

It seems that no matter what view we take on this topic, some lines of Scripture or facet of experience or evidence of God's image leaves us perplexed. Perhaps we should understand that, as a matter of principle, ultimate things must be left to the wisdom and discretion of God. Perhaps we have not sufficiently surrendered our own wills and egos and given ourselves to Him so that we are content whenever our understanding becomes clouded to simply "let God be true, but every man a liar!"

We may in our frailty and fallibility be incapable of keeping a "right judgment in all things" with respect to God's holiness, on the one hand, and God's love, on the other. Certainly the classic theologies have tended to stand against one another with regard to one or the other of these truths. Yet since God is both holy and loving, there must be a way of reconciling the one with the other. It may be that we shall have to leave the understanding of that reconciliation to the time when we shall join the multitude of heaven crying out, "Hallelujah! Salvation and glory and power belong to our God *for his judgments are true and just.*
. . . Hallelujah! For the Lord our God the Almighty reigns" (Rev. 19:1, 2, and 6, emphasis mine).

The reconciliation of the love and justice of God must not come by ignoring hell or believing that God is so good-natured that He does not care about moral character. The days in which we live are too serious for such sentimental trips. Such a view is a miserable misrepresentation of God who is of purer eyes than to behold iniquity. Such a view could never account for God so loving the world that He gave His only begotten Son that whoever believes in Him should not perish but have everlasting life.

Whatever ultimate destiny God assigns to each of us must satisfy both God's unutterable hatred of sin and His inexpressible love for us men. I dare to suggest that this is where we must leave any questions to which we cannot find entirely satisfactory answers in either God's Word or

Christian experience.

We can assuredly know that when the new heavens and the new earth are completed we shall be able with God to look upon everything that He has done and to say, as He said when He finished His earlier creation, "Behold, it is very good." In the meantime, our primary concern must focus on the present: "Today, when you hear his voice, do not harden your hearts. . . . Behold, now is the acceptable time; behold, now is the day of salvation" (Heb. 3:7, 2 Cor. 6:2).

9

HEAVEN:
THE GLAD FINALE

The word "heaven" is used in a variety of senses in both the Old and New Testaments. We are concerned with it in this study only as it is used to designate the destination of the saints. The Scriptures are silent on many things concerning heaven over which Christians generally, and theologians particularly, have speculated, studied, and argued through the centuries. The Bible gives us a large, general view of heaven as the final home of God's servants with its rewards of varying kind and degree corresponding to the gifts, character, and service in one's earthly life.

Negatively, heaven's blessedness is found in freedom from all sin and pain and sorrow. Positively, it promises throughout all time to come the depths of satisfaction to be known in sharing the very life of God Himself. This will include the attainment of all that has been reserved for us in heaven, which we have known only in a vague but tantalizing prospect called hope. It will also include the unfolding before us of all the manifestations of the eternal love and glory of God. It will bring to maturity for us all that is good as epitomized in the presence of Christ, "that where I am you may be also" (Jn. 14:3). The concept of heaven necessarily leaves much to the sanctified imagination so that even the Apostle Paul with his inspired and magnificent command of language could do no better in speaking of "our glorification" than to resort to a quotation from Isaiah: "Eye hath not seen nor ear heard, neither have entered into the heart of man, the things which God hath prepared for them that love him" (1 Cor. 2:9, KJV; *cf.* Is. 64:4).

In spite of the difficulty involved in trying to understand the glories of heaven, we may deserve the rebuke which one author levels at all Christians who do not sufficiently try to imagine the goodness and greatness of the things God has in store for us. In reponse to our distrust or dullness, J. Paterson-Smyth says:

Oh, this beggarly faith, that God has put up with, that treats the Father above as it would treat a man of doubtful character! "I must have His definite texts, I must have His written pledges, else I will not believe any good things in His dealing." That is our way. We talk very piously about our belief in God's love, but we are afraid to infer anything, to argue anything from the infinitude of that love. No, we must have God's bond signed and sealed. I do believe that one reason why we have not more of direct answers about the mysteries of the future life is because God thought that no such answer should be necessary — that His love, if one would only believe in it, is a sufficient answer to them all.[1]

Strangely, confidence in such a grand finale for the upright is shared not only by Judaism and Christianity but by many non-Christian religions as well. Do these convictions found in pagan scriptures attest to some sort of primitive knowledge that reaches back to man's creation in God's image — an instinct which, no matter how overladen, has not been completely eradicated or lost? Listen to these statements taken from the sacred writings of non-Christian religions:

(1) From the world's longest epic, the Mahabharata, originating in India probably as early as 800 BC, and from which has been extracted India's best loved devotional book, the *Bhagavad-gita:* "The great souls of departed saints, look ever down on earth, and are full of beauty, shining each in its own glory."

(2) From the Zend-Avesta, the sacred book of the Zoroastrians, from approximately the 6th century BC: "The righteous in heaven are undecaying and immortal, unharmed, undistressed, and undisturbed. Everywhere they are full of glory, fragrant and joyful, full of delight and full of happiness."

(3) From the Katha Upanishad, a "bible" of Hinduism from before 400 BC: "In the heaven-world there is no fear; thou are not there, O Death, and no one is afraid on account of old age. Leaving behind both hunger and thirst, and out of the reach of sorrow, all rejoice in the world of heaven."

(4) From the scriptures of Taoism comes this statement of Chuang-Tzu of the 4th century BC: "He who knows the joy of heaven has no grievance against heaven and no grudge against men; he is unembarrassed by things, and unrebuked by the spirits of the departed."

(5) And finally from the Koran, the sacred book of Islam, compiled in the 7th century AD from the revelations of the prophet Muhammed: "But announce to those who believe and do the things that are right, that for them are gardens 'neath which the rivers flow! So oft as they are fed therefrom with fruit for sustenance, they shall say, 'This same was for our sustenance of old.' . . . Therein shall they abide for ever."[2]

Since Christianity is based only upon the revelation of the Judeo-Christian Scripture, we will attempt now to trace briefly the development of the concept of heaven as found there. The Old Testament conceives of heaven as a region above the earth which is the dwelling place of God, but it is presented chiefly in relation to its divine majesty, remoteness, and holiness. The Old Testament scarcely treats heaven as the future inheritance of the righteous, focusing mainly on the present life. The consummation it expected was to take place upon the earth.

The New Testament takes over the general Old Testament idea but with certain enlargements and differences. It assumes that heaven is a region above the earth in that it speaks of the angels of God ascending and descending in relation to earth (Jn. 1:51); the Apostle Paul mentions having been "caught up" to the third heaven (2 Cor. 12:2); the Apostle John reports seeing a door opened in heaven and hearing a voice saying, "Come up hither" (Rev. 4:1), and he speaks of the holy city descending from God out of heaven (Rev. 21:2). The prayer our Lord taught His disciples begins, "Our Father who art in heaven," which adds to the Old Testament ideas of majesty, remoteness, and holiness, some new connotations of security, grace, and love. The whole conception of heaven as the dwelling place of Deity is made more appealing, tangible, and warm by its being presented as the scene of the present activity of Christ. Since Christ's earthly birth, life, death, resurrection, and ascension, heaven is much more "domesticated" and conceivable than it could have been before.

In certain large and significant passages, the cosmic and eschatological implications of heaven are suggested. In Romans 8, the apostle speaks of a redemption of the whole creation from the bondage of corruption. In Acts 3 the time of the restitution of all things is mentioned. Ephesians 1:10 and Colossians 1:20 tell of a gathering together and a reconciliation of things in heaven and on earth. The Apostle John also mentions a day when all things shall be made new (Rev. 21:5). Indeed, he is joined by Peter who writes of the formation of a new heaven and of a new earth in which righteousness dwells (2 Pet. 3:12, 13; Rev. 21:1).

The New Testament associates this renewal of the heavens with Christ's second coming and the final judgment. It connects the hope of a new scene and order for man's life with that of the final perfection of his life. Heaven in the New Testament is the final home of the righteous, the ultimate place which Christ is preparing for His followers (Jn. 14:2), the place from which He will come with His holy angels (Mt. 24:30) for the final rectification of all things and into which His own shall be received so that "where I am, there they may be also (Jn. 14:3).[3]

By this time you must be struggling to comprehend even a few of the implications of what is being said. Move over, please — for the writer is struggling with you!

To illustrate the difficulty we are encountering, imagine a person of good hearing, average intelligence, and mature years who has been blind from birth. Now exert yourself to the limit of your creativity in search of a way to convey to such a person the nature of the color green!

Imagine a similarly handicapped person who can see but has been deaf from birth. How would you attempt to give that person some idea of the majesty of Handel's "Hallelujah Chorus"?

God evidently has a similar problem in His attempt through His Son and the Bible to convey to us the glory of heaven. It is small wonder that John, in one attempt (Rev. 21:4), goes about it by listing a series of things heaven will *not* include! And then when he continues his attempt by describing the water supply and the fruit trees and the building materials of the walls, and the like, it turns out to be little better than the pictures of sensual bliss found in the Koran! We must remember that the reality about which he is writing is something far more than the literal meaning of the words used.

Heaven is the ultimate outcome of the eternal plan in the mind of God from the beginning. As a play or a painting exists in the mind of the artist before it is ever written or painted, with every problem solved and every contingency provided for, so the whole drama of redemption was fully formed in the mind of God before the foundations of the world were laid. Nothing that has happened since has altered or hindered the ultimate and glorious conclusion of it all, just as God had designed it.

Now at last Christ "shall see the fruit of the travail of his soul and be satisfied" (Is. 53:11). Just as at the end of His creative acts "in the beginning" He looked upon what He had called into being and said, "It is good," He shall look upon His victory accomplishment and know that it was worth the unspeakable cost:

— worth the incarnation of His eternal Son,

— worth the separation, the sorrow, and the pain of man's unbelief and hatred,

— worth being misunderstood, shamed, mocked, scourged, spit upon, crucified, and buried!

We have little capacity or vocabulary for describing what heaven will be like. Perhaps the moments of ecstasy known to those in love is a hint. Perhaps the unspeakable joy of a filling

137

by the Holy Spirit comes even nearer. But both of these together only illustrate the degree to which our limited and sensate faculties are ill-equipped to conceptualize the glories of heaven. In fact, our Lord suggested that just such comparisons were inadequate when He said, "When they [people] rise from the dead, they neither marry nor are given in marriage, but are like angels in heaven" (Mk. 12:25). The Apostle Paul illustrated the problem when he attempted to speak of his own experience of being caught up into the third heaven and could only say that he "heard things that cannot be told, which man may not utter" (2 Cor. 12:4).

An affluent people such as we are know full well how unsatisfying even the best of material things can be. The prospect of golden streets, gates of pearl, and beautiful thrones and crowns are hardly appealing, though surely they might have been in an earlier day when so many of the believers experienced relative poverty. But we do know that the child of God who has lived here in an earthly body, and in the near hereafter continues to exist in the spirit, shall at the dawn of the far hereafter be reunited again to a glorified body. These three stages of our life may indeed be described as good, better, and best!

Heaven is both something within us and something outside of us. The internal glimmerings of heaven which we experience during this life may be alluded to in the statement of our Lord that "the kingdom of God is within you" (Lk. 17:21, KJV). Our preparation for heaven begins with our regeneration. It progresses as we grow in Christlikeness, as we respond to the Spirit's activity in our lives and allow Him to mold us in the image of God who created and redeemed us.

Heaven surely refers as much to character as to location or rewards. "For the kingdom of God is not food and drink but righteousness and peace and joy in the Holy Spirit" (Rom. 14:17). Our direction is not a consequence of fate or accident but of our own choice or failure of choice. If God could send all men to Paradise and have them still be men in His own image, all men would surely be there. God does not withdraw from us our right to choose even though it would be for our own good. If God could keep all people from Gehenna, and still live up to His intention in creating humankind, no one would go there. It is character that makes either heaven or Gehenna and both of them begin here in this life.

Too often I have met persons during hospital visitation who indicate that they are going in the direction of torment by the fear in their faces, the profanity on their lips, and the desperation of their actions. Their decease on the operating table or during their hospitalization only propels them into the next life in the same direction they were going here.

But I have just as often, thank God, visited persons who gave every indication of traveling in their last days and hours in the direction of that happy presence with the Lord which awaits the righteous. Their facial expression was peaceful and expectant and their death a welcome release from the shackles of a broken-down body.

We have all, I suppose, heard discussions on whether heaven is a place or a state. Never forget it — it is both, and the *state* begins long before we reach the *place*, for the state is a matter of direction and attitude. Outward heaven can have little mearning until the inward heaven has begun to take shape within us. The trademark of our life has to do not with what we profess externally, but with what we are internally. It is a question of whether we have spiritually put on our wedding garment before we seek entrance to the marriage feast! (See Matthew 22:11-14.)

The purpose of the gorgeous vision of heaven is not to dazzle us with its bright rivers, sparkling thrones, white robes, great high walls, twelve gates, golden reeds, and precious stones constituting, surrounding, and undergirding a holy city. Rather, it should cause us to examine whether we have been partaking of the water of life, and putting on the robe of Christ's righteousness by our faith and obedience, so that we may be eligible to participate in the songs and music and feasting in the kingdom of God. (See Mark 10:29, 30.) This language makes sense to one who has tasted the good things to be known and enjoyed as Christ's disciple, but to the brutish, selfish person it is so much nonsense. A worldly person has been too preoccupied with temporal, selfish interests on the assumption that hard cash and worldly success are what count. You cannot prove to such a man that the joy of Christlike character with a conscience free of guilt is, in itself, any reward at all, since he has never given any attention to developing an appetite for the things of the Spirit of God.

All who have again and again sensed something of the deep reward of doing what is right and good, and rejecting the temptation to gratify themselves, bearing trouble for the sake of another, contributing to another's happiness, pushing on in doing the right at a considerable cost to themselves, have made a deposit in the kingdom "where neither moth nor rust consumes and where thieves do not break in and steal." They will eventually reap their reward when the books are opened and the judgments declared. *These* are the treasures. All the other tangible assets of this life we shall discover have no value or use in the life to come. Our Lord constantly reminded people that they could have their reward here-and-now or there-and-later. (See Matthew 6:2, 5, 16, 19-34.)

What will heaven be like anyway? To begin with, heaven is a place of residence. Surely we should not get hung up over the use of spatial terms even if the reality we are trying to speak of is supra-spatial. John A. T. Robinson's philosophical quibblings in *Honest to God* notwithstanding, it seems both unnecessary and impossible to disconnect the idea of locality from our conception of heaven. While it may well be that this whole concept relates more significantly to *being something* than to *going somewhere, i.e.,* that it is more a state of character than a place of residence, yet it may very well mean the latter as well. At least we in our humanity can scarcely think or speak of it in any other manner. It belongs to the condition of our present mental life and experience to think of heaven more or less in terms of locality, whether we think of heaven as the place where God is, or as the future home of beings like ourselves. Perhaps our conceiving of heaven as a place is further supported by the fact that our Christian faith teaches not mere immortality of our spirit but the resurrection and glorification of our body as well.

The chief joy of heaven will undoubtedly be what has been called the Beatific Vision. If we are completely honest, probably few of us are ready to say with Philip, "Lord, show us the Father, and we shall be satisfied" (Jn. 14:8). Most of us are not so heavenly-minded that we can say we desire to see God above all else. I admit that at this point my expectation of seeing God is mixed with the happy prospect of meeting loved ones, fellowshiping with great Christians of earlier times, and satisfying my curiosity concerning other features of the heavenly realm. But it appears that our becoming "like him" (1 Jn. 3:2) will chasten and purify our sense of values so that our priorities will be all that they ought to be. Once that has come to pass, our prime joy will be simply to live in the presence of God. All other joys will be

142

quite secondary much as the joy we experience in receiving a gift frequently derives more from our relationship to the giver than from the intrinsic value or usefulness of the gift itself. Our Lord Himself hinted at the deep joy which lay ahead when He declared that He would not drink with His disciples again until He would do so with them in the kingdom of God (Mt. 26:29). At that time He shall move among us as a great Servant, for we are told that in heaven His glory will be manifested to us even while He wipes all tears from our eyes! Apparently even in glory the greatest one is He who serves.

Second, heaven will be a time and place of worship. Here again we are given only a few tantalizing hints. The entire opening part of Revelation 19 is devoted to a scene of worship in heaven (vv. 1-8). The thunderous chorus of "a great multitude in heaven" (v. 1) is described as saying "Hallelujah! For the Lord our God the Almighty reigns" (v. 6). In response to the voice from the throne (v. 5) calling the vast congregation to "Praise our God, all you his servants," there comes heavenly music. Revelation 5:9 speaks of a new song that is to be written and sung and 14:3 tells us that the redeemed from the earth are to learn a new song. Some scholars see as many as fourteen fragments and stanzas of song recorded in Revelation alone — more than is to be found in any other book of the Bible except the Psalms! I have heard complaints from some Christians who are not intrigued by the idea of spending eternity in praise and worship. Perhaps Joseph Kenneth Grider relieves this fear when he suggests: "So while there is to be on the part of the redeemed a continuous worship in heaven, it seems to be in the sense that all activities engaged in will be for the glory of God and will therefore partake of the nature of worship."[4]

Third, heaven will be a place and time of service. Revelation 22:3, KJV, contains a most significant brief statement regarding the activity of those in glory. It says simply, "His servants shall serve him."[5] Earlier in speaking of those "who have come out of the great tribulation [and] have washed their robes and made them white in the blood of the Lamb," we read, "they . . . serve him day and night within his temple" (7:14, 15). The word is the same one used by the Apostle Paul when speaking of the service Christians render to their Lord in this life.

Fourth, there will be a sharing of authority in heaven. In several of our Lord's parables He speaks of assigning authority to His faithful servants upon His return. In the parable of the pounds, He gives to two of His servants authority over ten cities and five cities respectively. (See Luke 19:17, 19.) In the parable of the talents He says to the two good and faithful servants, "I will set you over much; enter into the joy of your master" (Mt. 25:21, 23). Nowhere is any further explanation given. There is simply this suggestion of authority and responsibility that is delegated to those citizens of the heavenly kingdom.

Fifth, there is the prospect of fellowship with

saints of other days. How many of us have had our hearts strangely warmed, as John Wesley did, by reading the writing of a Christian who lived long before us. Somehow a warm sense of fellowship transcends the time and distance separating us. I met a Christian once who told me he was particularly fond of the writings of John Woolman, the great Colonial Quaker witness. I admit a particular yearning to fellowship someday with Christopher Dock, the early American Colonial schoolmaster. I know of no Scripture verse to quote in substantiation of this drawing of heart to heart that occurs through the printed page and between the centuries and millenniums, but I cannot believe that it is out of order to surmise that the privilege of face-to-face fellowship will be ours in heaven.

In the sixth place, I suggest also that we will grow in knowledge after we get to heaven. So many things have puzzled us about the Lord's will as we have experienced it. This has been compared to the confusion of threads which one sees on the underside of a tapestry in contrast to the beautiful design on the front side. Well, I'm eagerly awaiting the opportunity to see the front side of God's design for the world and for His people. We sing, "Someday we shall understand." Surely it will delight the Lord to open to us the glories of His wisdom regarding past ages and future ones to come.

Finally, there shall be in all of heaven's perfection the rest which God has promised to His own. The Book of Hebrews speaks so eloquently of this: "For if Joshua had given them rest, God would not speak later of another day. So then, there remains a sabbath rest for the people of God; for whoever enters God's rest also ceases from his labors as God did from his. Let us therefore strive to enter that rest, that no one fall by the same sort of disobedience" (Heb. 4:8-11).

With such prospects of surprise and luxury and design and majesty and power and wisdom prepared for those who love God, how diligent we should be in dedicating our whole life to the attainment of that goal! Christ spoke of the merchant who, in seeking valuable pearls, found one and proceeded to sell all that he had to buy it! We must earnestly ask ourselves what we must do and what kind of persons must we be if we are to be present "when the roll is called up yonder." The New Testament guides us unerringly to that goal. It begins with repentance for our sins, believing on the Lord Jesus Christ, and then living moment by moment in obedience to His Spirit and Word and in fellowship with His church. It is not an easy road, but it is possible to follow it by the strength which God supplies throughout this life and right on into the next. By God's grace, I'll expect to see you there!

10

PROBATION IN
THIS LIFE

Have you ever thought of this life as a probationary period? Are you willing to think of it in this way? Does it offend you or does it intrigue you to think of this life in such a manner?

True, you had no choice in the matter of whether or not you were to be conceived and brought to birth. That for all of us is a "given." As for being a sinner, you need not even accept the "conceived in sin" (Ps. 51:5) doctrine as a universal explanation of sinfulness. We must not blame it on Adam either, as though we are unjustly bearing the brunt of the sin of our ancient forefather, for the prophet Ezekiel (chapter 18) tells us in no uncertain terms that we are not held accountable for another's sinfulness, but rather "the soul that sins shall die." The fact is that quite apart from the sinfulness of our parents, recent or ancient, we have sinned ourselves and find ourselves sinners. We discover that our entire personality with its desires, mentality, attitudes, and willfulness is fundamentally inclined to do the sinful and selfish things.

147

So without stopping to philosophize on *when* or *how* we got this way, we cannot deny this fact.

Without attempting to pinpoint the time or deed or place when all of us lost our innocence, we shall simply acknowledge that it is true. Indeed, even in the innocence of earliest childhood we were bundles of selfishness and greed, though we were not held accountable for our sins or sinfulness until we were aware of our own condition and capable of deciding for or against sin, self, and Satan. And now whether pursuing the way of Christ or that of self and sin, we are most assuredly on probation.

This need not be a burdensome or meddlesome fact for us. Rather, it can be a challenge to us of a most comprehensive and fundamental kind. It can be a necessary, indeed welcome, goad to help us keep on the "straight and narrow." For while we want to respond out of higher motives than simply to "save our own skins," yet the forgiveness and salvation which Christ will give us as a present reality is not without its conditions so far as our abiding in Him and doing His will are concerned. And while our salvation is not at all of works, "lest any man should boast," yet if it is genuine, it will manifest itself as a maturing factor in our lives — moving us toward Christlikeness.

Our Lord gives us ample warning against overconfidence concerning our salvation. We could discover at the last moment that Christ will say to us, "I never knew you; depart from me" (Mt. 7:23). It is important to keep in mind

148

that our present earthly life is a critical and probationary period of our unending life.

I do not believe in unconditional eternal security. I am convinced by Scripture, however, that everyone who has chosen Christ as his Lord and Savior and walks in Christ's will and way in fellowship with other Christians has nothing to fear so far as his salvation is concerned. Indeed, John's first epistle tells us that we who love and serve Christ "abide in him, so that when he appears we may have confidence and not shrink from him in shame at his coming" (2:28). John further says that as we love, not in word or speech only, but in deed and in truth, we shall know by this "that we are of the truth, and [may] reassure our hearts" (3:19, 20). These verses speak to the fact that our feelings (hearts) are not an entirely trustworthy guide to our spiritual condition. John then says, "If our hearts do not condemn us, we have confidence before God" (3:21), in which case we do not need external assurance to rest upon. However, since our hearts are rather fickle and sometimes condemn us even when they need not, we may be assured anyway for "God is greater than our hearts."

What do we mean by *probation?* In our discussion here, we will use the definition of Paterson-Smyth: "Probation in this life simply means that in this first stage of his being, a man either is or is not blinding his eyes and dulling his ears and hardening his heart so as to make himself incapable of higher things in the life to come."[1]

There is a great law of life that we must identify before going further. This law shall either be a great encouragement to us or a chilling warning, depending upon how we relate to it — whether with compliance or defiance! It does not mean that the consequences are irreversible either for our salvation or punishment since "with God all things are possible" (Mt. 19:26), but it does mean that the consequences of our choices are significant both for this life and for the life to come. The law we speak of may be stated simply: *Character tends to permanence*. Whether we realize it or not, our lives are fashioned by the decisions, thoughts, actions, and attitudes of our day-to-day living. Unless we choose to respond to God's offer and give ourselves unconditionally to His grace and mercy, we shall get what we deserve.

The awesomeness of this law may be illustrated by the career of Oscar Wilde. Wilde had a brilliant mind and won the highest academic honors. He was an unusually gifted writer, receiving some of the highest awards in literature. He was a person of great personal charm and basically kind, yet he fell to the temptation of unnatural vice and ended up in prison and disgrace. He wrote a book while suffering for his fall in which he said: "The gods have given me almost everything. . . . Tired of being on the heights I deliberately went to the depths in search for new sensation. What the paradox was to me in the sphere of thought, perversity became to me in the sphere of passion. I grew careless of the lives of others. I took pleasure where it pleased me, and passed on. *I forgot that every little action of the common day makes or unmakes character*, and that therefore what one has done in the secret chamber, one has someday to cry aloud from the housetop. . . . I ended in horrible disgrace" (emphasis mine).[2]

Some theologians tend to see the idea of probation as only partly biblical. They believe the concept "contains the conviction that this life is incomplete in itself and that man is continually under the eye of the eternal God. Insofar as it expresses the truth that 'God will render to every man according to his deeds' . . . (see Rom. 2:6-16) . . . the theory of probation is biblical. But when the Bible speaks specifically of God's probation it is chiefly a testing of his own elect with a view to confirming in their faith, not a general probation of all men."[3]

This definition of probation comes close to splitting hairs. Surely this life *is* incomplete in itself. And certainly the presence of the serpent in the Garden of Eden constituted a kind of probation or testing for the first pair.

Others, including myself, see probation throughout the Scripture even though it is never spoken of by such a term. R. J. Hammer alludes to Job's suggestion that suffering has a probationary, if not even a redemptive, quality. *The Jerusalem Bible* renders Job 36:15, "The wretched, however, he saves by their very wretchedness, and uses distress to open their eyes." The Scriptures' way of speaking of what we are calling probation is illustrated by such a passage as Judges 2:22 — 3:6

151

where the Israelites are beset by the surrounding nations "in order to test Israel by them, whether they will keep the way of the Lord to walk in it as their father did or not" (NAS). Hammer further believes that in such passages as Psalm 49 "there is a hint that in the world to come the incongruities of this world will be put right. Present existence is but an incomplete episode, and so seeming inequalities will not be fully resolved in this life." Indeed, if the word probation is understood to simply acknowledge the fact that God's ultimate purpose is not fully achieved in this life, then there is no question but that this life is probationary for all mankind! (Consider 1 Timothy 5:24, 25, and 1 John 3:2.)[4]

Furthermore, the Scriptures make clear that God's providential care is worldwide and indiscriminate to some degree. God's gifts are not carefully distributed with respect to "just deserts." Certain inequities are inevitable. (See Matthew 5:45 and Luke 13:1-5.) The probationary aspect of earthly life is strongly suggested also by such passages as "for you know that the testing of your faith produces steadfastness" and "Blessed is the man who endures trial, for when he has stood the test he will receive the crown of life" (Jas. 1:3, 12; *cf.* 1 Pet. 1:17). Peter's writing would further tend to refute the narrowing of the idea of probation to only God's elect when in his epistle (4:17) he says: "For the time has come for judgment to begin with the household of God; and if it begins with us, what will be the end of those who do not obey the gospel of God?"

We are saying that acts form habits, and habits determine character, and character points to destiny. Christian teaching has long held that this life is *the* probation time for mankind. The Scriptures imply this clearly. Paul in 2 Corinthians 5:10 says, "For we must all appear before the judgment seat of Christ, so that each one may receive good or evil, *according to what he has done in the body*" (emphasis mine), and this is the consistent tenor of Scripture.

The awesomeness of this fact is underscored when we compare the brevity of this life with the unending life to come. No wonder Paul is able to speak of the trials and sufferings of this life, no matter how great, as but a "slight momentary affliction" (2 Cor. 4:17) or as "not worth comparing" (Rom. 8:18) to the endlessness of life to come. Paul uses such phrases in reference to the glory that is to be revealed in Christians. Those headed for perdition face a frighteningly different prospect! Clearly, God's reward for our choosing to follow Him in this temporal life bears no proportionate relationship to the good things He has in store for those who will be with Him throughout the ages to come. It is particularly this facet of eternity to which the New Testament would point us. But it cannot emphasize only the positive since man has been given freedom to choose to go his own way if he will. This sobering fact accents again the probationary nature of our present life.

This, however, does not answer many of the hard questions for which we long for more light.

153

For one thing, for a probation to be fair and genuine as we view it, the person must know that he is under trial and what the consequences are of his failure to meet the reasonable expectations. The customary view does not speak to the special cases of retarded mental development, or the mentally ill, or of those primitive people we often call "the heathen," or yet of these millions now and in the past who never in their dreary, dingy lives had any fair chance of knowing the Lord in a way that might have prompted them to love Him. How can we help but wonder about the eternal destiny of such persons? Answering that God is utterly righteous and not willing that any should perish is consoling but not entirely satisfying. What we are saying in this case is that since we do not and cannot know God's intention with such persons we must be content with the confidence that the Judge of all the earth shall do right (Gen. 18:25), as Abraham believed.

Our Lord declared on one occasion (Mt. 11:23) that had the mighty works done in Capernaum been done in Tyre and Sidon, they would have repented! Does this suggest that He will make allowance for those of Tyre and Sidon in some other way, or what? The Calvinist has a ready answer. Since all men deserve to be damned we can only praise God for those whom God chooses to redeem! This provides cold comfort at best, and less than that if you happen not to be among those chosen! Must we not assume that the Lord will do

154

as much for all who would have loved Him if they had had an opportunity to know Him as He has for us who do have such knowledge and opportunity? We are not speaking of those who have had rich opportunity to know the Lord and may have even served and followed Him for a period of time only to have drifted into a state of indifference, if not rebellion, against the Lord. Rather, we are thinking of the spiritually underprivileged.

The possibility in this life of putting ourselves outside the reach of salvation is awful enough without our making it worse. Surely Christ is not displeased that we should earnestly search for every smidgen of knowledge that may help us to come to a better understanding of this matter. If "God so loved the world that he gave his only Son, that whoever believes in him should not perish but have eternal life," and we are made in His image, then we may be expected to raise the question, even if we are not granted a fully clear answer.

We know that it is *willful choice*, not knowledge or good works, that determines one's destiny. God alone can righteously evaluate that choice and one's subsequent life. All the subtle influences which go to make character are known to God alone. We keep making discoveries in this area but are only dipping our toes into the vast ocean of human personality and potentiality.

The solemn thought remains that the probation of this life seems to be the determining factor in human destiny for all mankind — even for the unthinking, the ignorant, and the heathen. The Apostle Paul lifts the veil for us a bit when he says, "When Gentiles who have not the law do by nature what the law requires, they are a law to themselves, even though they do not have the law. They show that what the law requires is written on their hearts, while their conscience also bears witness and their conflicting thoughts accuse or perhaps excuse them on that day when, according to my gospel, God judges the secrets of men by Christ Jesus" (Rom. 2:14, 15). Paul implies here that the man who does not have opportunity to know, much less consciously accept Christ, determines during his earthly life by his response to whatever imperfect light of conscience he has what his response will be in the next life toward Him who is the light of the world. That man, like all of us, is forming on earth the moral and spiritual bent of his future life.

The Scriptures seem to imply that all men in all lands and in all ages have received light to some degree and that each person's attitude and response to whatever light he has, determines on earth his direction in the hereafter. He is forming character and character tends to permanence. The outer darkness comes not from absence of light but from willful choice.

It appears that it is possible for even a heathen person to have in this life sufficient light, however poor or fragmentary, to guide him however dimly to God and that he will be judged, not according to God's fullness of revelation in Christ and the Scriptures, but according to whatever understanding and insight the man had received and was capable of responding to with his gifts and in his environment. The Apostle Paul, in his message to the pagan Lycaonians who began to worship him and Barnabas, said: "We also are men . . . like . . . you, and bring you good news, that you should turn from these vain things to a living God who made the heaven and the earth and the sea and all that is in them. In past generations he allowed all the nations to walk in their own ways; yet he did not leave himself without witness, for he did good and gave you from heaven rains and fruitful seasons, satisfying your hearts with food and gladness" (Acts 14:15-17).

I cannot escape the indelible impression left on my mind and heart in reading a compilation of excerpts from American Indian literature from earliest days to the present. I found a variety of evidences illustrating just what Paul said God has always done among all men everywhere. Let me cite several examples:

(1) A young chief of the Cayuses said in an Indian Council in the Valley of Walla Walla in 1855: "The ground says, The Great Spirit has placed me here to produce all that grows on me, trees and fruit. The same way the ground says, It was from me man was made. The Great Spirit, in placing men on the earth, desired them to take good care of the ground and to do each other no harm."

(2) Brave Buffalo, a Sioux Indian (born in 1838), said when he was 73: "When I was ten

years of age I looked at the land and the rivers, the sky above, and the animals around me and could not fail to realize that they were made by some great power. I was so anxious to understand this power that I questioned the trees and bushes. It seemed as though the flowers were staring at me, and I wanted to ask them, 'Who made you?' . . . Then I had a dream, and in my dream one of these small round stones appeared to me and told me that the maker of all was Wakan tanka (Great Spirit), and that in order to honor him I must honor his works in nature.''

(3) A chief among the Blackfeet upon being asked to sign one of the first treaties in his region of the Milk River in northern Montana said: "We cannot sell the lives of men and animals; therefore we cannot sell this land. It was put here for us by the Great Spirit and we cannot sell it because it does not belong to us.''

(4) Red Jacket, a Seneca Chief, said in 1824 concerning his opposition to the Christian missionaries: "We cannot read their book — they tell us different stories about what it contains, and we believe they make the book talk to suit themselves. . . . The Great Spirit will not punish us for what we do not know. He will do justice to his red children.''

(5) Powhatan, a ruling chief in the Virginia territory, said in 1607 to Captain John Smith: "Why will you take by force what you may quietly have by love? . . . What can you get by war? . . . We are unarmed, and willing to give you what you ask, if you come in a friendly

manner, and not with swords and guns, as if to make war upon an enemy. . . . Take away your guns and swords, the cause of all our jealousy, or you may all die in the same manner."[5]

Enough quotations! The point is that there is much indeed that can be known of God and responded to in simplicity and reverence even outside the revelation of God in His Son and in His Word. And the further point is that as our Lord said, "Every one to whom much is given, of him will much be required; and of him to whom men commit much they will demand the more" (Lk. 12:48b). Those of us gifted with the knowledge of both Christ and the Scriptures are not permitted the luxury of ignorance (if such it is), but are rather the more seriously on probation to respond with a fullness of love and earnestness to the privileges and obligations that our favored life has given us.

Free will is a glorious but frightening prerogative. We may all our lives, upon the impulse for some immediate advantage, select sinful and selfish alternatives only to discover that our character has been so warped and hardened into an evil shape that we enter into life, if at all, "maimed or lame" (Mt. 18:8), as our Lord said. Though the Bible does not answer all our questions by any means in relation to the subject of this chapter, it can be said clearly that the whole trend of its teaching leads us to the impression that this life is our probation time. Everywhere and with utmost earnestness the Bible calls us to immediate repentance. It is

159

as though the Scriptures know something about the future that we do not and perhaps cannot know which prompts it to speak with such urgency in calling us to repentance and righteousness.

The warnings are ominous: "The door was shut" (Mt. 25:10); "for it would have been better for them never to have known the way of righteousness than after knowing it to turn back from the holy commandment delivered to them" (2 Pet. 2:21); and "Behold, now is the acceptable time; behold, now is the day of salvation" (2 Cor. 6:2). These call us to prompt response in this dispensation with the ominous implication that such an opportunity cannot be assured in any other. Whatever new discoveries of God's power and mercy may await us in eternity we cannot know. But from all we do know, we can only urge with the utmost earnestness that men confess their sins, accept the offered forgiveness, and give their life unstintingly to Christ's obedience. If anyone does not do this, and risks his chances on some future turn of events, he is being utterly reckless and foolhardy. Surely God could scarcely even in the life hereafter overlook any such utterly perverse and selfish attitude. We dare not underestimate what the love and patience of God may do, but neither dare we presume in the face of Scripture to lighten the awful responsibility which this life affords.

One facet of this responsibility is the command of our Lord to "go into all the world and preach the gospel" (Mk. 16:15), For all of the blunderings and inconsistencies to be found in the history of Christian missionary effort, it does not follow that "ignorance is bliss" and that therefore those peoples who have never heard the gospel are better off in their primitive innocence than they would be if the message of the life and death of Christ were preached to them. Christ has not left that conclusion to our judgment. For the very love which brought Christ to earth from heaven is shed abroad in all Christian hearts also so that we are impelled to give our lives to that ministry which God Himself initiated in Christ. He covets our willing, loving response to the fullness of His revelation. Christians will always be under orders to share the good news of Christ's redemption and grace with all mankind. The heathen are not to be left in their ignorance even in cases, rare as they are, in which they may have come to near-Christian insights and response. We will be guilty of the same despicable sloth and lovelessness as the man who buried his talent if we do not take bold measures to invest the good news in a needy world. Our failure to do this will bring upon us only the sternest words of rebuke and punishment from the Lord. (See Matthew 25:14-30.)

"He who testifies to these things says, 'Surely I am coming soon.' Amen. Come, Lord Jesus!" (Rev. 22:20).

NOTES

Chapter 1

1. I have confined my citations here to the New Testament. There are three similar cases in the Old Testament: the son of the widow of Zarephath (1 Kings 17:17-24); the son of the Shunammite couple (2 Kings 4:18-36), and an unnamed dead man who was cast atop the bones of Elisha (2 Kings 13:20, 21).

2. William Shakespeare, *Hamlet*, Act III, Scene 2.

3. Alan Richardson, ed., *A Theological Word Book of the Bible* (New York: Macmillan Co.), 1951, p. 60. Brackets mine.

4. Richardson, *ibid.*, says, "The notion of some kind of penal connection between sin and death is focused in such prophetic teaching as Ezek. 18 ('the soul that sinneth, it shall die'). . . . Nor does the Old Testament encourage the sentimental notion that death is 'natural,' a necessary aspect of the ordering of nature; on the contrary, death is evil (Deut. 30:15, 19). . . . The fact that it is all these things is in some way connected with the fact that (like sin) it is alien to the divine nature and is no part of God's original intention in the creation."

This is simply a typical statement of the common and traditional evangelical Christian view and seems not to attempt to discover in the first place whether the reference is to physical or spiritual death, and, in the second place, conspicuously bases its conclusions on Old Testament Scriptures.

5. That death is alien to God's original intention may seem to be supported by the passage in Revelation 20:13, 14, where "death and Hades" are twice mentioned, first as giving up their dead, and second, as being thrown into the lake of fire, which action is described as the second

death. This obviously cannot mean that all who have died are to be cast into the lake of fire, for it speaks, just prior to these lines, of those whose names are in the book of life. Furthermore, the phrase "death and Hades" seems clearly to be redundant and a double personification alluding particularly to those whose names are not in the book of life. Verse 15 clarifies that this personification pertains only to the wicked dead.

The first death for the wicked is their spiritual alienation from God whether in life or in death and this second death is their final and complete separation from God. Perhaps most significant of all is verse 6 of this same chapter which says: "Blessed and holy is he who shares in the first resurrection! Over such the second death has no power. . . ."

Chapter 2

1. *Jewish Encyclopedia*, Vol. XI (New York: Funk & Wagnalls, 1907), p. 282.

2. *Ibid.*

3. *Ibid.*, Vol. IX, p. 515. Of the three users in the Old Testament of the word "Paradise" each is rendered as follows in the RSV: "orchard" in Song of Solomon 4:13; "park" in Ecclesiastes 2:5; and "forest" in Nehemiah 2:8.

4. Quoted by Paterson-Smyth, *The Gospel of the Hereafter* (London: Hodder & Stoughton), 5th ed., pp. 30, 31.

5. Only here in all the New Testament is Hades used when Gehenna would seem to be what was meant — unless, of course, Jesus saw no reason to make this distinction in order to convey His point.

6. I am indebted on these points to articles in two encyclopedias, one by Dwight M. Pratt in James Orr, *et al.*, *The International Standard Bible Encyclopedia* (Grand Rapids, Mich.: Eerdmans' Publishing Co.), 1946, Vol. I, p. 282; the other by Everett F. Harrison in *Baker's Dictionary of Theology* (Grand Rapids, Mich.: Baker Book House), 1960. p. 492.

7. Paterson-Smyth, *op cit.*, p. 44.

8. *Ibid.*, p. 55.

Chapter 3

1. There is, of course, another possibility. Our progress toward Christlikeness might end with our death. Although we would be "with the Lord" in the afterlife, yet the com-

pletion of our sanctification would somehow be completed at the second coming of Christ. By this view, the intermediate life would simply be a waiting life. I proceed along another line of thought, however, in this chapter.

2. Ruth Montgomery, *A Search for Truth* (New York: Bantam Books, Inc., 1969), pp. 71-73.

3. Alfred Edersheim, *Sketches of Jewish Social Life* (Boston: Bradley & Woodruff, n.d.), p. 117.

4. Arthur Chambers, *Our Life After Death* (London: Charles Taylor, 1905), p. 92, emphasis his.

5. *Ibid.*, p. 94.

6. A. H. Strong, *Christ in Creation and Ethical Monism* (Philadelphia: Roger Williams Press, 1899), p. 421.

Chapter 4

1. *The New Schaff-Herzog Religious Encyclopedia*, Vol. III (Grand Rapids, Mich.: Baker Book House, 1950), p. 182. See also articles in *Mennonite Encyclopedia*, Vol. I, p. 137, "Apostles' Creed" and in *Baker's Dictionary of Theology*, ed. by Everett F. Harrison (Grand Rapids, Mich.: Baker Book House, 1960), p. 131 f.

2. Paterson-Smyth, *op. cit.*, p. 111.

3. William Barclay, *The Letter to the Hebrews* (Philadelphia: Westminster Press, 1957), p. 195 f.

4. John Wick Bowman, *Layman's Bible Commentary* (Richmond, Va.: John Knox Press, 1968), p. 81.

5. Charles A. Trentham, *Broadman Bible Commentary* (Nashville, Tenn.: Broadman Press, 1972), p. 85.

6. J. B. Phillips, *Ring of Truth* (New York: Macmillan, 1967), pp. 118, 119.

Chapter 5

1. James Stewart, *Evangelism Without Apology* (Grand Rapids, Mich.: Kregel, 1960), p. 49.

2. See the article, "Resurrection," in *Jewish Encyclopedia* (New York: Funk & Wagnalls, 1908), Vol. X, p. 382.

3. *Ibid.*, p. 385.

4. Thomas Babington Macaulay, Essay on Ranke's *History of the Popes*, 1839.

5. Arthur H. Compton, *The Freedom of Man*, 1935, quoted by Woods, *The World Treasury of Religious Quotations* (New York: Hawthorne Books, Inc., 1966), p. 465.

6. Ray Summers, *The Life Beyond* (Nashville, Tenn.: Broadman Press, 1959), p. 31.

7. See the article, "Resurrection," in *Baker's Dictionary of Theology* (Grand Rapids, Mich.: Baker Book House, 1960), p. 448.

8. *Ibid.*, pp. 448, 449.

Chapter 6

1. I wish to acknowledge my considerable indebtedness for much in this chapter to several articles in Hastings two-volume *Dictionary of Christ and the Gospels* (Edinburgh: T. & T. Clark, 1913), particularly to those entitled "Advent," "Coming Again," "Parousia" by G. M'Hardy, "Character" by A. Norman Rowland, and "Prophet" by Charles T. P. Grierson.

2. James M. Stayer, *Anabaptists and the Sword* (Coronado Press: Lawrence, Kan., 1972), pp. 246-248.

3. G. M'Hardy, *op. cit.*, Vol. I, p. 343.

4. Elton Trueblood, *The Future of the Christian* (New York: Harper & Row, 1971), p. ix.

5. G. M'Hardy, *op. cit.*, "Parousia," Vol. 2, p. 322 f. This quotation must not be taken to suggest a separation between Christ's own words relative to His return and those teachings given in the other New Testament writings, as though the former is superior to or in conflict with the latter. We do not believe such to be the case, but we chose not to go into this matter any more extensively at this point. The Book of Revelation does represent a special kind of literature quite unlike either that of the Gospels or the epistles, but there also the thrust of the teaching is not at variance with that given by our Lord.

Chapter 7

1. See J. Burnier's article, "Judgment in the New Testament," in Von Allmen's *Companion to the Bible* (New York: Oxford University Press, 1958), p. 211, and R. Martin Pope's article, "Judge, Judging," in Hasting's *Dictionary of the Apostolic Church* (Edinburgh: T. & T. Clark, 1915), Vol. 1, p. 661.

2. Hastings, *ibid.*, W. Morgan's article, "Judgment, Damnation," p. 661. J. Oswald Sanders in his booklet, *How Lost Are the Heathen?* (Chicago: Moody Press, 1972) cites two evidences of this coexistensiveness: Celsus, the Greek philosopher of the second century, in a treatise against Christianity, asserted that "from of old it was the universal belief that the wicked shall suffer endless pains" and an

ancient Chinese proverb says, "Good has a good recompense; evil has an evil recompense. If you say there is no recompense, it is because the time has not yet arrived" (p. 46).

3. Arnold C. Schultz in *Baker's Dictionary of Theology* (Grand Rapids, Mich.: Baker Book House, 1960), article, "Judge, Judgment," p. 303, emphasis mine.

4. B. Martin Pope, *ibid*, p. 660.

5. N. H. Snaith's article, "Judge, Judgment," in Richardson's *A Theological Word Book of the Bible* (New York: Macmillan, 1951), p. 118.

6. J. Burnier, *ibid.*, p. 213.

7. Nathan E. Wood's article, "Judgment," in *Dictionary of Christ and the Gospels* (Edinburgh: T. & T. Clark, 1906) Vol. 1, p. 914. I am indebted to much in this article concerning the point under discussion. He lists some of the tests given by our Lord as follows: "Following Him (Mt. 4:18-22, 10:38, 19:28, Mk. 8:34); confessing Him (Mt. 10:32, Lk. 12:8); failure to appreciate His presence and work (Mt. 11:2); failure to come to Him (Jn. 5:40); failure to believe Him (Jn. 3:18); failure to obey Him (Jn. 3:36); failure to honour Him (Jn. 5:23); failure to stand with Him (Mt. 12:30); failure of right fruitage (Mt. 21:31-42, 7:16, Lk. 6:44); failure in outward conduct (Mt. 22:11-13); failure to help men (Mt. 25:31-46); failure to repent (Jn. 5:40); failure to use the gifts of God (Mt. 25:14-30); making light of His personal invitations (Mt. 22:1-7); unwillingness to hear His words (Mt. 12:41, 42); unwillingness to forgive an injury (Mt. 6:15, 18:28-30); being ashamed of Him (Mk. 8:38); breaking a commandment (Mt. 5:19); the spirit of our judgment on others (Mt. 7:2); faith or lack of it (Mt. 8:10, 9:22-29, 15:28. Mk. 5:34); heart unreceptive to His words (Mt. 10:14, 15); hypocrisy (Mt. 23:13-36); idle words (Mt. 12:36); lip service without the heart (Mt. 15:7); selfish conceit (Mt. 6:2); wicked pride (Mk. 12:38); love of darkness (Jn. 3:19); rejection of His disciples (Lk. 10:10); adultery (Mt. 19:9); commercialism in worship (Mt. 21:13); blasphemy against the Spirit (Mt. 12:31, 32); loving others more than God (Mt. 10:37); hearing, seeing the Son, with belief or with failure to believe (Mt. 7:24, 13:23, Jn. 5:24, 6:40); the cup of cold water given to a disciple (Mt. 10:42); mercifulness (Lk. 6:36); love to Christ (Lk. 7:47, Jn. 21:16); love to enemies (Lk. 6:27); humble-mindedness as a child (Mt. 18:4); fidelity of service (Mt. 20:14, 24:45-51); endurance in well-doing (24:13);

doing will of God (12:50); deeds in general (16:27); inward thoughts and motives (Mk. 7:21, Lk. 5:22, 23)."

8. According to this system, the "sheep and goats judgment" is to take place on earth and is God's judgment upon the nations; "the judgment seat of Christ" event takes place in heaven during the seven years of great tribulation on the earth and is a judgment on believers; "the great white throne judgment" takes place in the air while the earth is being purged by fire at the end of the millennium and is a judgment upon the wicked of all ages.

9. If Paul intends this phrase to be understood as broadly and as unqualifiedly as it stands, it is a striking statement indeed! It seems to support the proverb that no one is so wicked but what some good can be found in him.

10. Quoted by J. Oswald Sanders, *op. cit.*, p. 54. Sanders' booklet is a stimulating, though not entirely adequate discussion of these questions. However, I wish to acknowledge my gratitude for the help received.

11. The counterpart to the question here under discussion is that the rewards given to the righteous will vary also as the parable of the talents suggests. (See Matthew 25:14-28.) The explanation for the differences in the amounts entrusted is that they did not have equal ability and therefore should not in fairness be expected to produce equally. Indeed, verse 15 says that the man distributed his talents "to each according to his ability." It is interesting to note that his statement of commendation to the two who were entrusted with the five and two talents respectively is identical, although the one talent taken from the slothful servant is given to the one who doubled his five. It may be inferred that each one shall be perfectly happy with his reward even though it differs from the reward of others since each reward will be in perfect harmony with the differences both in the gifts given and in the ability to put them to good use.

12. Cited by Sanders, *op. cit.*, pp. 50, 51, from the writings of S. D. F. Salmond in *The Expositor's Bible*.

Chapter 8

1. A dramatic illustration of this is found in Psalm 119:147, KJV. "I prevented the dawning of the morning. . . ." This is quite an undertaking! This verse simply means the psalmist arose before sunrise but the

modern meaning of prevent suggests that he stopped the sun from coming up! A similar misunderstanding is possible in 1 Thessalonians 4:15, KJV, where the Apostle Paul is saying that those who are alive on the earth when the Lord returns shall not prevent those who are asleep, meaning only that the living shall not be caught up to meet the Lord before those who will be resurrected are enabled to do so also.

2. Taken from *Mishnah Torah*, 1170. E. H. Plumptre in his commentary on Mark's Gospel in the *Ellicott's New Testament Commentary* series (London: Cassell & Co. Ltd., n. d.), pp. 141 f., says in reference to 9:44 that these words "do not absolutely exclude the thought that the fire may consume or destroy, in the sense of annihilating, that which it cannot purify; *still less do they affirm that it will.*" (Emphasis mine.)

3. Woods, *op. cit.*, p. 211, an excerpt from Montefiore's book, *Liberal Judaism*, published in 1903.

4. In correspondence with Dr. Leon Morris of Ridley College, University of Melbourne, Australia, concerning the problems posed by the historic evangelical view in light of passages such as this, I received the following reply:

"The problem of universalism is a difficult one. I appreciate that there are some evangelicals . . . who can discern the importance of preaching the gospel even if all men will be saved in the end. But I do not think that people will carry on vigorous evangelism if they feel that men are going to be saved anyway. Perhaps I am unduly influenced by my own personal laziness. But I cannot envisage myself being a strong supporter of a missionary society or evangelistic crusade if I really thought that in the end the same object would be attained if nothing were done. So I cannot go along with the universalistic premise.

"I realize there are two groups of universalists, those who sit loose to Scripture and those who accept it. Among the latter I have from time to time met people who can make out quite a good case, using the passages you mention and also a number of others. But human nature being what it is, I cannot think that evangelistic endeavor can flourish where universalism is consistently held. None of the arguments of my friends have been able to convince me of this."

5. Alan Richardson, *A Theological Word Book of the Bible* (New York: Macmillan, 1951), p. 107.

6. Charles T. P. Grierson, *Dictionary of Christ and the Gospels* (Edinburgh: T. & T. Clark, 1913), Vol. 2, p. 441. Grierson undoubtedly alludes to such passages as 1 Timothy 2:4; 2 Peter 3:9; Hebrews 6:7, 8, John 12:31 f.; Luke 3:6; Titus 2:11; 1 Timothy 4:10; I John 2:2; and 1 Corinthians 15:22-29.

7. Let me acknowledge again my indebtedness in this discussion of New Testament words and concepts to the book mentioned earlier by J. Paterson-Smyth.

8. J. Paterson Smyth reports this investigation without citing the source or sources except to quote a summary statement by a Dr. Dewes to be found on page 23 of *Pleas for a New Translation* for which Smyth gives no publisher, date, or place.

9. J. Burnier, "Judgment," *Companion to the Bible,* ed. J. J. von Allmen, (London: Lutterworth Press, 1958), p. 213 (my italics).

Chapter 9

1. Paterson-Smyth, *op. cit.*, p. 224.

2. Quotations taken from Ralph L. Woods, *The World's Treasury of Religious Quotations* (New York: Hawthorn Books, 1966), pp. 425, 426.

3. For this all-too-brief summary, I am indebted to S. D. F. Salmond's article, "Heaven," in Hasting's *Dictionary of the Bible* (New York: Charles Scribner's Sons, 1909), Vol. 2, p. 323.

4. Joseph Kenneth Grider, in the article, "Heaven," *Baker's Dictionary of Theology* (Grand Rapids, Mich.: Baker Book House, 1960), p. 265.

5. In support of the quote by Grider just given, this verse is translated in the RSV as "his servants shall worship him."

Chapter 10

1. Paterson-Smyth, *op. cit.*, p. 142.

2. Quoted by William Barclay, *The Letters to the Galatians & Ephesians* (Philadelphia: Westminster Press), 1958, pp. 116, 117.

3. Harrison, *Baker's Dictionary of Theology* (Grand Rapids, Mich.: Baker Book House), 1960, article "Probation" by Donald W. B. Robinson, p. 421.

4. Alan Richardson, *op. cit.*, article "Suffer," pp. 248-253.

5. McLuhan, *Touch the Earth* (New York: Outerbridge & Dienstfrey), 1971, pp. 8, 16, 53, 63, and 66 respectively.

INDEX OF
SCRIPTURE REFERENCES

172

GENERAL INDEX

175

179

180

181

GERALD C. STUDER is pastor of Plains Mennonite Church, Lansdale, Pennsylvania, and author of a biography, *Christopher Dock: Colonial Schoolmaster*, and *Toward a Theology of Servanthood*.

He is president of the board of trustees of Christopher Dock Mennonite High School, Lansdale, Pennsylvania, and a member of Franconia Mennonite Conference Council. He is coeditor of the historical quarterly, *Mennonite Historical Bulletin*, and of *The Bible Collector*.

Studer has been a member of the Mennonite General Board with headquarters at Lombard, Illinois, and has contributed articles to many periodicals and journals. He served two previous pastorates, at Smithville, Ohio, and Scottdale, Pennsylvania.

He has the Master of Divinity degree from Goshen Biblical Seminary, Elkhart, Indiana. He has a Bible collection of rare editions and different versions totaling over 1,800 volumes.

Gerald Studer was born on January 31, 1927, in Smithville, Ohio, and is married to the former Marilyn Kreider, Wadsworth, Ohio. They are the parents of two daughters, Jerri and Maria.